Come! Come! Where? Where?

Also by James Seay

Come! Come! Where? Where?

James Seay

ESSAYS

The University of North Carolina Press
CHAPEL HILL

This book was published with the assistance of
the Fred W. Morrison Fund of the University
of North Carolina Press.

Designed and set by Lindsay Starr in Dante MT Pro
Manufactured in the United States of America

Cover art: Bird illustrations, courtesy of Adobe.

Some of these essays, in different form, appeared in
Antaeus, Blackbird, Carolina Quarterly, Esquire, Harper's,
the *Independent Weekly*, and *Oxford American*.

Library of Congress Cataloging-in-Publication Data
    Names: Seay, James, 1939– author.
Title: Come! Come! Where? Where? : Essays / James Seay.
Description: Chapel Hill : The University of North Carolina
    Press, [2024]
Identifiers: LCCN 2023034111 | ISBN 9781469678139 (cloth ;
    alk. paper) | ISBN 9781469678146 (paperback) |
    ISBN 9781469678153 (ebook)
Subjects: LCSH: Seay, James, 1939– | Seay, James, 1939—
    Family. | Poets, American. | Southern States. |
    Southern States—In literature. | LCGFT: Essays.
Classification: LCC PS3569.E24 C66 2024 |
    DDC 808.84/9975—dc23/eng/20230824
LC record available at https://lccn.loc.gov/2023034111

FOR LUCY AND SPENCER

Contents

Come! Come! Where? Where?

Down among the Bones, the Darks, the Sparrows

There are the Boones too, maybe kin to the Bones, and the Lloyds, the Merritts, the Rigsbees. Old Carrboro families my son is among in the under-earth. When I can free myself of the grief of his death, it amuses me to think of my Josh entering that dominion, him strange to them in his ways and from unfamiliar family, not of their place. But with a sweetness and bravery and wry smile those folks could not long fail to accept and allow into their fold.

At the moment, a bee is testing a plastic flower at the base of Josh's gravestone, then it moves on to the asters, marigolds, Russian sage, and rosemary I have brought to his grave today. The honey to be made of the dead, the blent nectar gathered among the flowers for the Bones, the Boones, Vonnie and Annie Horton, Darian Earl Bryan dead in a car wreck at thirty-nine, his portrait in oval porcelain, the Darks, the Sparrows.

Camber is that subtle, slight rise of an arch in favor of support for what is above it. The man who was the project manager for the building of my house pointed it out to me before the sheet-rockers covered it. Camber. Laminated beams, cambered and bearing the weight of my bed above. You can see it on I-40, whatever is your interstate. Tractor trailers, eighteen-wheelers, long open trailers cambered most freely when they are deadheading, bound for home with no load. Free-bedded. The camber there like a waiting angel. At an angle from Josh's grave is the Woodcock/Camber grave. I don't know the family, Woodcocks, Cambers, but Josh is among them. One of the truths of fatherhood, not knowing how balanced is a son's full weight in the world, or, in Josh's case, how his illness lay on the given camber.

Josh is buried at the end of a row of graves running parallel to the backmost road of Westwood Cemetery. His mother Lee and I shared the duties of putting him to rest. She asked if I would find a burial plot for his ashes. The cost of a plot in the old Chapel Hill Cemetery, even if one could find a family willing to sell a space there, was beyond reason. I went to the town hall in Carrboro, the adjacent town where Josh once lived and where he worked in Lee's sushi restaurant, and I found that there were available plots in Westwood. On the map there was a space, serendipity, at the end of the row parallel to the back road. And it turned out to be beneath a tree.

That is where my dog Neville and I are today. Neville, a she, goes straight for the October pumpkin next to Josh's grave. Sniff, sniff. And then on to other graves. Bones, Darks, Sparrows. My guess is that Lee has left the pumpkin, along with a flower arrangement.

I empty the water from the little plastic music-box piano that was left on Josh's gravestone shortly after his burial. It is a small-scale grand and has a profile of Elvis on the top. It used to play "Love Me Tender" when wound up. After a few rains it could barely plink out Elvis's plea, and then it gave up. But it's still there in its mysterious provenance. When I first found the piano, I called Lee to see if she put it there, but she said no, she thought

I had. To this day, we have no idea who beyond family summoned our son's love. And counted on that summons being heard. Two graves down, on the Butterfield grave, someone has left a scale model Corvette, top down, headed east toward Josh. Maybe the Butterfield boy is taking Josh for a ride. I don't know. As Brando, perhaps aware of St. Peter's similar question, asked his lover in *Last Tango in Paris*, "Quo vadis, baby?"

Wheat Field with Crows

AUTHOR'S NOTE: The massacre at Sandy Hook Elementary School set me to thinking of our children and the world they occupy with us. Added to my grief over the deaths in Connecticut was my fear that the mentally ill would be further stigmatized. And we would have failed as parents and pilgrims on the path we share with them. In contemplating this, I do not know why I was put in mind of the trip to New York City with my son Josh before the onset of his mental illness. But it was not a stretch to then think of how all this related to his illness, his strength and courage in that illness, and how it is harmful in the extreme to place the mentally ill in a single grouping, to see them all in a negative cast, to deny that we all stand in the same light. Though sadly there are some who stand at times in darkness. Those thoughts led to this essay.

Before 9/11 you could ascend the tower at Riverside Church on Christmas Eve and view the carillonneur as he offered Handel's *Messiah* to the world within hearing. Whatever your faith or none, the hymnal he summoned from the seventy-four bells and twenty-ton Bourdon had to arouse something deep and spiritual in your being. How turn away from that wordless chorus? Hallelujah, הַיְוּלְלָה, alleluia.

My son Josh and I were there in 1986, a birthday trip to New York City on his seventeenth, a year before the onset of the mental illness that eventually took his life. But on that day we were "lit up," as he would say, full of the joy of the season and our good fortune, father and son, at being together 400 feet over Riverside Park on the afternoon of Christmas Eve and having our eardrums pounded with Handel's proclamation of "the magnificence of the lord God omnipotent reigning forever."

That is not to say we were totally lost in the spiritual ether. We could not take our eyes off the Asian woman standing alongside us at the window of the Clavier Cabin. Softly intent on the carillonneur, she would have been a Zen cliché had it not been for her coat, a riot of crimson against her black hair, and her butterfly bow, whimsical and silver in the winter light. When she turned from the carillonneur, her eyes were shut, perhaps in transport or rapture. Or maybe simply to assuage the light glancing off the river. Josh nudged me and directed my gaze to her hands resting on the railing. They were exquisitely formed. I think Josh intended for me to note that quality as well as the absence of a wedding ring. The slight tilt of her head, eyes still closed, accentuated the delicate flaring of her nostrils. It was as though she were searching the chill air for something. But what? Something we could never imagine, Josh and I agreed when discussing it later. As a father I was intrigued by how that tincture of sensuality and interiority seemed to register with Josh. He was a handsome boy, a musician in his own right, putting in hours at the piano—Pachelbel, George Winston, Prince's *Purple Rain* his favorite—playing and singing with his band, and forming an intellectual sense of the world. Throughout his schooling Josh scored very high in standardized testing. And none of us had a hint of the illness that would beset him in the coming year.

On the preceding day we had been to the van Gogh exhibition at the Metropolitan, *Van Gogh in Saint-Rémy and Auvers*. Van Gogh in the final fifteen months of his life. Following an argument with Gauguin, van Gogh sliced off the lobe of his left ear and delivered it to a prostitute in the local brothel. Soon afterward he voluntarily entered the asylum at Saint-Rémy. There he completed some 100 drawings and 150 paintings, including *Starry Night*. The stars in the night sky rage and spiral, seeming to strain toward nuclear fission. Mediating between that energy, that disquiet, and the quiet of the village—innocent, one assumes, of anything that could be visited upon it from above or within—are the church spire and the cypress, which thrusts even higher into the starry night. What are we to make of those twin thrusts? A bargain for equilibrium? A plea?—don't let me cut off my other ear.

Equally dramatic and more ominous is the painting *Wheat Field with Crows*. It was painted only a few days before van Gogh's suicide, and there's a good chance it was his final painting. Van Gogh had left Saint-Rémy in 1890 and gone to Auvers-sur-Oise to be near his brother Theo and fellow painters. In the center of the painting a road divides the field but has no obvious destination other than the storm-ridden sky into which the crows disperse and blend. The crows lack any quality of avian grace and loft. Their flight is heavy and carries a strong suggestion of fatal consequence. Was that the *suggestio veri* that Josh and I looked for as we studied the paintings?—an intimation that van Gogh was soon to do further violence to himself? Or to others? And could anyone have intervened? As we left the museum and made our way up Fifth Avenue, Josh and I puzzled also over the cipher of the hand that guides with such passion the brush in its limning of the world and the next day lifts a gun to revoke that world.

But the bustle of Christmas was all around us, and soon we were caught up in a spirit of merriment, joking and making plans for our continued blitz of the city the next day. As we passed East

Eighty-Sixth, I pointed out a Carnegie Hill neighborhood sign and told Josh to ask me how to get to Carnegie Hall. "Okay," he said, sensing I was jiving with him, "how do I get to Carnegie Hall?" "Practice, practice, practice," I answered. Such a tame and dated joke, but you would have thought I was *Saturday Night Live* personified the way Josh broke up laughing, and then we started clowning back and forth. But I did let him know that Carnegie Hall was not in the Carnegie Hill neighborhood; rather it was in Midtown Manhattan, and now he would know how to get there when they invited him to play his piano in concert. "I didn't get the directions very well," he said, "tell me again how do I get to Carnegie Hall?" And we both shouted out in unison, "Practice, practice, practice!!!"

At Fifth and East Ninetieth, a homeless man had unplugged the lights on the Christmas tree outside the Church of the Heavenly Rest and plugged in his hot plate. He was heating something in a pot, beans or Campbell's soup or maybe Sterno to strain through a cotton sock for the hit of alcohol it would give him. Josh and I slowed to get around his sidewalk kitchen and then picked up our pace toward our friend Roy's apartment across Central Park at Ninety-Sixth and Broadway.

It was there, up a few blocks, that we had our Christmas dinner the next day at noon. Sushi and sashimi and multiple cups of sake. We talked again of van Gogh, the hand holding and at the same time letting go. We talked of the photographs we might have taken—I had raised my camera once and then let it drop unshuttered as the Asian woman lifted her closed eyes to the Hudson. We talked about the homeless man, how his hand too was holding and at the same time letting go. That paradoxical embrace of the world that one has already relinquished.

The plan after our orgy of raw fish and sake was to go downtown and get on the ferry to the Statue of Liberty. When we got to the ferry station, we learned that the ferry to the statue wasn't running on Christmas Day. We threw up our hands in dismay. But then we turned and there were the Twin Towers. We were on the observation deck of the South Tower in a heartbeat.

At about fifty-five minutes into the 2002 *Spider-Man* movie, you can see the Twin Towers reflected in Spider-Man's eyes. He is climbing up a building on a mission to save the city. That reflection was evident in the original poster for the film, but after 9/11 the image was removed. A similar occlusion occurs in *The Sopranos*. Before the attacks, the towers can be seen in Tony's side-view mirror in the opening credits of each episode. Alabama 3 is singing "Woke Up This Morning" (*You woke up this morning / Got yourself a gun. / Mama always said you'd be / The Chosen One*), and as Tony leaves the Lincoln Tunnel and enters the Turnpike on his way to his home in New Jersey, we get a glimpse of the towers. That view is an impossibility in real life, but the transgression of borders, whether geographical or moral, including Tony's savagery and disregard for human life, is a signature element of the show. (And considering the iconic status of the show, it is an element to which our imprimatur as a culture is clearly affixed.) After 9/11, though, the towers have been removed from Tony's drive home.

On our departure for home, Josh and I are waiting in our seats on one of the planes of the nearly bankrupt People Express airline. It is New Year's Eve, and we want to be home for my birthday on New Year's Day. Our flight has been delayed on the tarmac for over an hour. We are waiting for a replacement part. A cart toodles up and the driver hands a cardboard box to the mechanic waiting under the wing of our plane. The mechanic opens the box. In one hand he holds up the faulty part he has freed from the plane, and in the other he holds the new part. He tests the heft of each and looks at the failed part and then at the part that is supposed to set us on our journey home. He continues to juggle the two, as though the heft will answer his question. Is this the right part? Can I get this tin can flying again? Josh and I watch out the window. The flight attendant tells us we can deplane if we wish and wait for a later flight. We decide to go with the new part, and we fly home.

Less than a year later my former wife Lee and I gave Josh over to the care of professionals. His was the classic onset in late teens

Wheat Field with Crows

of schizoaffective disorder. We finally found a combination of medicines that gave him a life. Josh was able to live alone in his condo, drive his cool black Toyota Spyder to work, and play the piano in Lee's sushi restaurant on Saturday nights. We found also a compassionate and keenly intelligent clinical psychologist who, in addition to weekly talk sessions, sometimes brought his alto sax to join Josh at the piano on weekends. Josh's was not the life of collecting Kevlar vests and rounds of ammunition for Bushmaster .223s. Nor was that the life of, say, his fellow workers at Caramore, one of our local rehab centers. They came with Josh to my yard and raked pine straw into neat piles for use in mulching. They pulled dead zinnia stalks from my garden and cut back the dried asparagus plants in preparation for the coming spring. Some of them looked at the wage money in their hands as though it were a curiosity. They loaded up the Caramore van with furniture I gave them and a Sony television for their group home. We stood around and drank Cokes, though many wandered off to smoke, one of the familiar ways that the mentally ill and recovering addicts mediate between life and chaos. Their plumes of smoke, thick and ascendant, were not unlike van Gogh's cypress reaching into the sky.

Don't get me wrong. I grew up in a family of hunters. My father had a hunting camp in Mississippi within five miles of William Faulkner's hunting camp. I own guns. But I am willing to do whatever it takes to bring us to a sane resolve.

A common side effect of the medicines Josh was taking is an inordinate weight gain. His heart gave out one night during his thirty-third year. The matter of the failed part on the People Express jet is not a metaphor I would push. But it is true that my son had no replaceable part, no matter the heft and efficacy of anything that could be found in his behalf. It is true also that Handel shook the stones where we stood above Riverside, and we thought of ourselves as lovers of the Asian woman. We tried to understand van Gogh and the homeless man with his hot plate, the hand holding and at the same time letting go. We walked out onto Broadway, warmed with sake and acting like twelve-year-olds—*practice, practice, practice*—and the light was the light of boulevards and fields held in the pledge of return. Planes circled in a wide holding pattern over LaGuardia as we looked out from the South Tower with no notion other than the joy of our moment there.

Wheat Field with Crows

The Weight of a Feather

Laura, who comes every other week to clean my house, seems not to engage with the little narratives I leave for her. On my refrigerator, for instance, I have three fish magnets that I arrange in a simple linear narrative, no *Last Year at Marienbad* or *Memento* stuff. At the top of the story is a fish I got in Barbados. It is a barracuda-looking fish. But if it is in fact a barracuda, it is one goofy-looking barracuda. It's just swimming along with no thought for the morrow—or, for that matter, the moment. Below it is a shark that I have set in a vicious downward angle in pursuit of what looks like a snapper, but it's not a red snapper, more blue and green. Probably a spangled emperor snapper, though the emperor when frightened will change its color, so who knows. The snapper is swimming desperately upward in the direction of the nitwit barracuda, but its attempt to escape is clearly doomed. The shark is hungry, relentless. Laura rearranges the fish in peaceful and parallel paths across what I intended as an ocean of pain and truth. I don't think she has a Disney World narrative in mind, but that's the story I see.

As I am a fisherman, several of my narratives for Laura involve the sea, the whale-roads of the ancients. Recently the captain of one of my shrimp boats, the *Pequod Junior*, rammed the boat into a rock formation. I left the boat lying awash and snagged on the rocks for Laura to discover. It was what sailors call "broke deep," its hull broken into below the Plimsoll line. The captain was unfamiliar with these fishing grounds, fog ruled the night, and the rock formation does not appear on any of the known nautical charts. This occurred in the otherwise safe waters of a shelf in my study. A larger trawler, the *Essex*, has just managed to veer away from the rock formation. The captain, a woman who has been with my fleet for years, saw the rocks just as she was about to set upon them and pulled hard on the ship's wheel. She is a recovering alcoholic, so this is not her first rodeo. In the far distance is a Greek lighthouse with a sweet little skiff, the Δαφνη, moored nearby. Daphne. None of my other ships are under Greek registry, nor is the Aegean the site of this occurrence. It's just that the maritime world of my shelf is vast. As for the disaster, Laura sets the *Pequod Junior* aright and goes about her dusting. I was hoping she would bring the Δαφνη over for a rescue mission. Or run the *Essex* aground, not that my female captain needs another shipwreck in her life.

More complex is the *tableau vivant* I arrange on a shelf in my bathroom. I say *vivant* here, but that is not to suggest that the fish magnets and shrimp boat captains don't have lives and agency in their world and mine. The difference is that the central figure on my bathroom shelf has a different claim on my life. At the center of the tableau is a fish. It is acid-etched into a small rectangular piece of granite. A Greek fisherman on Mykonos gave it to me. He was also a restaurant owner and womanizer. I was in his restaurant with my then-wife, and he was drinking wine and holding forth at a table of fellow fishermen nearby. Full of wine myself, I stopped by his table to say that I was a fisherman also. He rose from his chair and embraced me and especially my then-wife in Zorba-the-Greek embraces. I was Alan Bates to his Anthony Quinn, but I don't quite know whose equivalent my then-wife was in this Mykonos movie. The fisherman insisted that we sit at his table and drink wine.

An hour or so later he invited us to see his art collection. That's where he gave me the granite fish. The only thing I could come up with in reciprocation was the small Buck knife I carried. He thought that I was reaching for money to pay him, and he threw up his large and calloused fisherman hands in veto. But when I extended the pocket knife in the palm of my hand, he accepted. He then began to make overtures to my then-wife and insist that we drink more wine. That's when I knew we needed to head for our rental car. As we departed, he took my hand in a handshake. Looking at me with eyes that scanned day after day Homer's wine-dark sea, he told me that he knew I was not a fisherman because my hands were soft.

Gathered around the Homeric fish on my shelf as though in worship are an elephant, an awe-stricken weasel, a sheep on a child's wooden alphabet block, a ceramic Scotch terrier, and three alligators. The alligators are wooden pencil sharpeners that my friend Jane brought to me from the Alligator River in eastern North Carolina. You put pencils in their mouths and they sharpen them.

In my narrative for Laura I take one of the alligators from its cohort of three and place it across the tableau to stand between the Scotch terrier and the sheep, though still facing the heroic fish. This alligator is the outlier, the alienated one, the contrarian, or perhaps the ostracized one. Or maybe even the joker. Those are possible agencies that I have not made clear in my narrative. Laura takes the lone alligator and places it back to make complete the alligator trinity, apparently the only configuration that she can imagine.

There is, however, a story in which we have a mutual understanding and investment. I had an exquisitely curved needle for the repair of bicycle tires in emergency situations. Not the tube, the tire. The shape of the needle's cross-section was not rounded; it was triangular, in favor of more flex strength. It had an extra-large eye to receive the thick linen thread needed for tire repair. I used the needle to string cayenne peppers from my garden. Not that I needed flex strength; I just wanted a needle easy to thread. I hang the peppers in my kitchen for chili and the Mexican dishes that cast my gringo stomach into hell. The needle turned up missing from its home, a bowl I bought from a man in Zihuatanejo. The bowl is magical with its fish and mermaids, who have only the one stylized eye on the side of the head, as is common in primitive paintings. There are palm trees and an ocean from which a smiling sun arises. My needle was a citizen in that prelapsarian world.

I suspected some painters who were working inside my home, and to put them on notice that I knew the needle had been taken, I asked Laura to write a note that I would leave displayed on the kitchen counter in hopes that one of the painters might surreptitiously return the needle to its bowl. *El señor*, she wrote, *quiere saber si ustedes uleron la aguja del estambre*.

My *aguja del estambre* was never repatriated. But I later figured out that it was not one of the painters who took my prized awl, rather it was their Anglo boss. At another time when he was completing a job in my house and was the only one with access, I came home to find a leather belt missing from the closet door knob where I had left it hanging.

His girth was notably larger than mine, though mine is not what you would call slight. What possible use could he have had for my belt? He's going to offer for sale on eBay a single belt? The story by which he could have found relative happiness in his life must have been lost somehow in a history of kleptomania, and he would forever seek in stolen items that lost narrative. But the son of a bitch had my *aguja del estambre* and handsome leather belt, and all I had was an empty bowl—still magical, but sombered by degree of its lost citizen—and the memory of a handsome belt which I wanted to keep me girded and distinguished when I walked out into the world.

At another time Laura sucked up into the vacuum cleaner an eagle feather that I had not told her the story of. Nor had I arranged it in any playful narrative for her to take up or fail to respond to. While staying in a wilderness lodge in Alaska my friend Jane and

I decided to get out of the wilderness and back onto the grid for a day or two. We went to see the calving of the Aialik Glacier. Great tons of ice calved into the water, and we were part of that thundering spectacle. Jane had found a small charter boat for us, and we had the whole bay to ourselves, just the four of us, the captain and his sweet wife and Jane and me. The two-story tour boats had gone in an opposite direction to view another glacier, but they were socked in, fog obscuring their view, they reported on the radio. Small isles of ice, luminous with a delicate blue cast, floated around our boat. The captain's wife broke one into pieces and packaged it for martini ice.

The captain told us that he had some work to do on the engine of the boat and he would put us ashore to view the Aialik up close. Handing us a canister of pepper spray, he said that grizzlies might come down from the upper elevation in search of salmon but the pepper spray ought to keep them at bay. Just don't get between them and the salmon. As Jane and I skirted the glacier, the captain shut down the engine of his boat, which now seemed diminutive and far away. Soon after the cessation of engine noise, we realized that there was no sound in the world except that of our own voices and the occasional calving of the glacier. We fell silent and listened to the only sound there was.

Something caught my peripheral vision, and I looked down to find a white feather, almost indistinguishable from the snow except for the slightly different coloration of the quill. My guess was that it was the feather of a bald eagle. One is ill-advised even to appear to have interfered in any way with the life of a bald eagle in Alaska. If the feds don't get you, the long mystical reach of the Inuit will find and haunt you in your dreams. But this was only a feather, which I later verified as that of a bald eagle by comparing it to the plumage of a mounted specimen in a museum in Homer, Alaska. A Homeric eagle, so to speak. I took it home.

I put the feather on the tray of a scale, one of a collection of scales that I have in a recessed section of shelves beneath the stairs leading to my study. What do things weigh? And of what value is that weight in the world? On one scale is an arrowhead I found in a field after a rain in my native Panola County in Mississippi when I was a boy. The arrowhead is probably Choctaw, of which blood I am one-sixteenth. After a rain in a freshly plowed field is the optimum time and place to search for arrowheads. The soil is washed anew, and the search is intensified by memory of one's few previously discovered arrowheads unearthed by the plow and glistening wet in the sunlight. The arrowhead on my scale has a unique opposing bevel, an enhancement that makes for a twist after penetration, a surer purchase in the flesh. That, its maker must have reasoned, would be the difference between eating mush for another week or making the kill and eating meat.

On a postal scale near the scale from which Laura's vacuum snorted my eagle feather like ethereal blow is a letter from Dmitri Nabokov responding to my request for directions to his father's grave in Montreux. "Enter by the main gate (rather than the one by the chapel) and, after passing, on your left, a large angel left over from an ancestor of ours, take the next lane on your right. Midway through, on your left, you will see 'Vladimir Nabokov, Ecrivain.'"

On another scale are the jaws of a beaver our guide John Herzer gave me when my friends Will, Duck, Vereen, and I were fly-fishing on the Bitterroot River in Montana. I put the jaws in a mild solution of bleach to cleanse them of desiccated flesh and whiten the bone, accentuating the tawny brown coloration of the teeth. The teeth of beavers can take down trees you wouldn't imagine. The curve of the teeth is almost exactly that of my lost *aguja del estambre*.

I should not have taken the pottery shard that I found beside a path on Delos in the Aegean. I had left the Terrace of the Lions and was walking to the peak of Mount Kynthos to look down on the birthplace of Apollo and Artemis. The pottery shard has the imprint of the human hand at work, part of an arc, and I can imagine the circle in the wet clay that the potter needed in order to make complete the story in her mind. It is balanced on its double-tray scale by a pottery shard from a path in New Mexico I shouldn't have taken either. But I imagined it as a gift from the Anasazi to the Choctaw.

On another scale there is a foreign bill from Czechoslovakia. My friend Jaroslav, who survived Dachau, wrote back to thank me for that portion of bills that I had sent him for Christmas. But the currency had been devalued. The governing currency now, he said, was that of the Czech Republic. With signature Slavic humor he told me that he had left the bills on Kafka's grave, weighted with little stones, the latter a Jewish custom. He and I had visited the grave the year before. When I stopped to buy a flower for Kafka from a street vendor, Jaroslav smiled and said no, no, no. He picked up a pebble and handed it to me. I was to place it on Franz K's grave, he instructed me. What do things weigh? What is the weight of a 100-koruna bill from a past ministry? Or the weight of a feather? Or the weight of a human body that has been reduced to almost nothing? Jaroslav told me he thought he would die in Dachau. When released and sent home to Prague, he ate raw liver, following a folk custom, to regain his life.

What narrative can I draw from the tonnage of history carried by these objects on my scales? A story of currency which once had value but now is no more than paper in the hand? That in some chamber of the human mind it is possible to reason fake shower heads that release Zyklon-B into the tiled room? And that my friend's name was not on the list for a shower and the incinerators? That an angel is transported with care from Russia to honor a grave in Switzerland? That in haste one day Laura sucked my eagle feather into the vacuum cleaner? And by the time I figured out what had happened, the dust bag was lost in a dumpster at the recycling center?

When my father, who sat beside me on the Caterpillar D8 bulldozer, reached and gently, though with unmistakable intent, took my hands away from the levers that controlled the direction of the bulldozer, I did not know what he was trying to tell me. What was the story? Then I reasoned that he meant I did not need to expend energy constantly adjusting the direction of the bulldozer. At the time, that was the only way I could understand his lifting of my hands from the levers.

We were in a large field, and I had the bulldozer headed in the general direction of where we needed to go. If required, radical turns of the bulldozer could be initiated by foot pedals, but short of that, the direction of the machine was controlled by the two steel levers that I straddled. Pull on the left lever, a slight braking action occurred in the left tracking system and the dozer tracked accordingly; pull on the right, similar response. But I was tending the levers with unnecessary attention to nuance. I was a teenager, and I wanted to show my father that I was a man who could operate this enormous machine he had entrusted me with. But it wasn't as though we needed the laser precision of a guided missile. We were easily headed in the direction of an area of the field where my father would give me further instruction in operating the large blade of the bulldozer. It lacked the hydraulic system of today's bulldozers. The blade was controlled by a steel cable coiled around a drum behind me. The lever extending over my shoulder engaged with the drum. Similar to the effect of the directional levers, if I pulled one way on the blade lever the drum took up cable and the blade lifted; pull the other way, cable was released and the blade lowered. What my father was instructing me in was the proper alignment of the blade with the earth or object that was to be bulldozed.

We were draining the Everglades. Or at least a portion. We didn't know any better, not that my father would have otherwise desisted. We were getting down to the rich soil beneath the water. Muck, it was called. Black and organic from centuries of decomposition of the richness the Glades had covered. It was unlike anything we had in the soil of Panola County, Mississippi, our home. That fecundity, in tandem with two growing seasons a year, possible in the warm climate of South Florida, made for ideal farming. Though, as with any farming, success is not a given. The farmer adjacent to us told me that just as he was readying for the harvest of his major iceberg lettuce crop of the year, a cloud appeared above his field. It was a square cloud, he said, a replica of his field, and it aligned itself with its earthly likeness. Hail came down out of it with a fury.

The Weight of a Feather

An anomaly in South Florida, but there it was. The farmer said it looked as though someone had walked down the rows and shot each individual head of lettuce with a Colt .45 pistol.

Before you indict us for our violation of the ecology, unwitting though it was, please consider that this was the 1950s. There was not the ecological awareness that there is today. Consider too the possibility that you have eaten celery, corn, lettuce, beans, and the like from that drained land. And sugar. The man who owned the land, and for whom my father worked, sold the land to exiled Cubans, who turned it to sugar cane.

To get to that soil, we had built a bridge across the West Palm Beach Canal and begun forming dikes and digging a network of drainage ditches. The drainage was accomplished by diesel engines powering pumps that drew the water into the West Palm Beach Canal. The pumps ran day and night, fed by elevated fuel tanks that we had mounted beside them. To control the flow of fuel, my father installed mechanical governors on the engines. But if we neglected to keep the fuel tanks properly filled, they would empty and the engines would go out of control, revving madly on the diesel fumes from the tanks. The governors could control only liquid; they lacked engineering to control fumes. If an engine was going to go berserk, it was inevitably at night. My father and I drove into the dark of the Everglades to try to shut down engines that would otherwise shake loose from their concrete foundations. Usually we could manage to shut them down, but on one occasion a renegade engine shook itself into heaps. Cougars came to the periphery of the field to see what all the commotion had been about. Their eyes shone in our headlights as we left the field.

And so when my father took my hands from the levers, I assumed that he meant for me to line up the dozer in the direction that we needed to go and not fiddle with the controls unless there was need to change course in an appreciable way. We were headed for an area of the field where the next day Desmond and I would be bulldozing willows and other vegetation from former hummocks. We would then push the uprooted trees and brush into piles and set them on fire. Sometimes just for fun, instead of using the dozer blade, Desmond and I would jam down on one of the foot pedals and spin around insanely on top of a willow to uproot it. An occasion for grand laughter in the heat that was otherwise almost unbearable.

Desmond was a Bahamian. He had come to Florida to earn money for his upcoming marriage to the woman who was waiting for him back in the Bahamas. He brought what he called sweet biscuits to the lunches we shared, just the two of us in that desolate expanse of open field. Anywhere we looked there was nothing. The black ground we had cleared extended into the horizon, flat with no relief. But Desmond talked of love. As a teenager, I had no story in which to incorporate what he said, other than to know that this woman was his life. One day he brought no sweet biscuits, ate nothing that I offered, and said that his woman had taken up with another man. We cranked up the dozer, made our piles, poured on them a mixture of diesel fuel and gasoline. Whoosh.

Desmond never regained his sense of play and buoyancy. Previously in situations where we differed in strategies for meeting an engineering problem, we would laugh it off and work half his way, half mine, or flip a coin. Now he would turn away and say, "Don't vex me, mon."

It was not until years later that I understood the story my father was trying to tell me in taking my hands from the levers. He was not arranging fish magnets and wooden animals and boats in play. He was not placing feathers on a scale. He meant that I should not infatuate myself with the Caterpillar tractor or the engines that drove the pumps or the notion that there would forever be another piece of earth to turn into arable land. He did not want me to follow his life. Or to let the power of the machine delude me into thinking that it was a power within my body. His kind of work, he wanted me to know, would finally break a body or put it at risk of injury. The latter of which would find truth in his own life.

While trying to help a man he supervised, he had bent to lend his hand to a large wrench the man was struggling with in breaking down a dragline for repair. Draglines were what we used in digging the network of drainage ditches that cleared our fields of water. They were Northwest draglines, I remember, because my father had a Northwest dragline watch fob that I coveted.

The wrench slipped and struck my father in the temple. A week later he blacked out on the way home from work. I was called to where our Willys Jeep truck was resting peacefully on the elementary school lawn, as though it had been given an unexpected recess. We drove my father to Palm Beach for surgery and then to Miami for further surgery to address the clot in his brain. He came out like James Brady, who took a head-hit in the assassination attempt on Reagan. My father became a man I barely knew. He laughed inappropriately. He cried when laughter would have been the normal response.

It is a commonplace to note that some of the stories we attempt to tell elude or otherwise fail in their mission. Likewise stories that we are told. We can't follow the narrative line; it escapes us utterly or we lose it somewhere along the way. Or the import of the story eludes us. As for the stories we tell, those that involve a sense of play are particularly prone to misinterpretation. They have the wrong traction, the wrong tonal register, the wrong timing. They can embarrass us or leave us unsatisfied with our attempt. On Wikipedia they would be in need of disambiguation. But we continue to offer those stories for play in the world. How else would Laura have the chance to bring the little Δαφνη across unimaginable nautical miles to the rescue of a broke-deep shrimp boat? Ah, Daphne, whom by our story we free from the laurel tree of myth to join us in rescue and then make jokes with us about the beleaguered captain of the *Pequod Junior*. How else laugh finally about a feather with a claim on sacredness getting sucked into a vacuum cleaner? Or about the fisherman who wanted to fuck my then-wife? How else not be lost in weeping for the hurt and the too-soon gone?

Through the Trees

The first hint of my mortality came to me through the trees in my grandparents' yard, but because I was young it was not a message that I could make any sense of. My mother and I were living with her parents in Senatobia, Mississippi, for there was a war going on and my father was in the Pacific with the First Marine Division, engaged in the invasions of Peleliu and Okinawa. Though those were two of the most savage amphibious assault campaigns in the war, it was not the message of that kind of death that came to me. It was of the ordinary kind, and it came to me at night through the trees.

My bed was beside a window that gave onto my grandparents' front yard, which was bordered along both sides and on the street front by tall cedars. They had been planted there many years before, and all of them had flourished in the straight and solemn fashion of proper cedars except for one on the street front that had been split by lightning and had healed with a lopsided fork in its trunk. A feature that distinguished it from the others, like the disabled veteran in the reunion portrait.

During the day the cedars held to their places, aligned and evenly spaced along the yard's borders. But at night they drew in around the yard almost as though they were trying to create a private darkness. Rising out of this assembly was a huge pine. It was in the center of the yard on the north side of our front walk. Memphis was north, I remembered, and the pine was on the Memphis side. Originally there had been a twin on the south side—the side toward my home, Panola—but the twin had been taken long ago by blight or pine beetle. The symmetry was lost, but in its place a notion of the traditional lonesome pine seemed to be more than enough compensation for my grandfather, who, before his stroke, often spoke of the tree in a tone suggesting that it offered profound messages that only he understood.

What he did not suspect, and what I was not aware of myself, was the message coming to me through the trees at night. It came at night because that was when Pate turned on the pale blue neon light running along the eaves of the porch of his house across the street, creating a powder-blue haze in the canopy of our cedars, which themselves had a blue-green tint in daylight. That haze at night filled the bedroom I shared with my youngest uncle with an even slighter phosphor of blue. The neon letters spelled C. O. PATE FUNERAL HOME, and I would fall asleep each night in the luminous blue glow of their effort.

A measure of hope would have been taken from me, I think, if the message had entered my life in an ambience of barrenness and inanition. As it was, the pale blue light came to me filtered and dispersed through the veil that spread itself outside my window: cedars, crepe myrtle, lonesome pine, and, in the summer, insect hum and the voices of my family on the porch. And in at least three seasons of the year, there was the wind that soughed through the trees at night with its own messages. Thus the insinuations from the blue tricking of tube-work above the entrance of the old family residence into which the mortician Pate had moved his marble slab were caught and gathered into the great stream that flows through our sleep, and I was not left with only that one irreducible blue image informing my dreams and shaping the inner narrative my life would draw on.

I am not suggesting that I was spared confusion. So little did I know of the world that for much of the time I did not know what was happening. I did not know why my grandfather retreated further and further into reticence and then had a stroke that took away his powers of motion and clear thought. I did not know that my mother's shifts of mood could be measured by the frequency of mail from the islands strung through the sea toward Japan. Nor could I fully understand the events my father referred to in the onionskin letters she read to me. Or know that the calmness of his tone—though provisional, I now realize—had been won in some place of the mind that had refused to be taken over by panic as the landing craft door dropped open.

Nor did I know why, when my grandfather called me to his bed and demanded that I return it, I so needed to keep the pocket knife he had given me the year before. I reminded him that he had given the knife to me before his stroke and had said that I did not have to share it with my cousins. Without acknowledging his breach, he repeated for me to go get the knife and bring it to him immediately. I told him a lie, saying that I had left the knife at my house in Panola when my father went to war and we came to live in Senatobia. I promised to get it when I was in Panola the next time. My excuse from then on, when he remembered to call me to his bedside and ask for the knife, was that I had forgotten it. Even now I do not know how I was able to deny him the knife he needed beside his bed before death. This was the man who took my mother and me in while my father was away, who once came home from the livestock auction with a young pig tucked under his arm for me, who rolled Prince Albert cigarettes and blew wisps of smoke into my ear when I had an earache, who rose in the winter dark to lay the fire that warmed the room for when we woke.

And so in that and other things I did not know what was happening. Once after I asked my Aunt Metra if I could play in her drawers in the family chest—I was fascinated by the objects there— she announced at the dinner table that "Jimmy wants to play in my drawers." She was smiling, and her announcement brought what I realize now were conspiratorial, though guileless, smiles around the table. I had the distinct sense that they had in mind something beyond what I meant, but I did not know what.

While that was a relatively mild experience, there were the more vexing moments of confusion surrounding that time in my life. Still and all, certain things I was sure of. I knew that my mother was sometimes solemn or fatigued from her job at the local ration board giving out ration stamps for gasoline, tires, sugar, chewing gum. And I knew that she was sometimes intent on deciphering the code my father used in one of his letters to let her know which island they were rumored to be headed for next.

Oh Lucie how I miss you. Know that I think of you and little Jimmy every day. I am doing okay, considering the rain that will not stop and the food they give us, or so it is called. No way will I ever eat Spam again. . . .

The sentences went on, the first letter of each being the code. With her map my mother could figure out that the next island would probably be Okinawa. How this easily broken code made it past the censors, I do not know. Many soldiers used much more elaborate codes in their letters home. But it wasn't as if the Japanese had not figured out that Okinawa was next after Peleliu. Later, when Okinawa was secured, my father sent a photo of himself in front of the shack he and his platoon had built from debris and the door of a bombed island temple. I'm sure that he thought that the next assault would be on Japan itself. But the bomb was dropped and he came home.

It occurs to me now that the wind soughing in the trees at night was an emblem of the confusion I felt. Its sound was not a whine or a moan, rather it was a whisper contradicted by a steady *shhh*, and I was certain that it was possible sometimes to distinguish between

the whisper and the *shhh* of the cedars and that of my grandfather's lonesome pine. One would whisper to me as I lay in the
deep feather bed beside the window, but before I could unravel its
syntax there would be its countervailing *shhh* or the other would
whisper and shush in the same breath and finally there was only a
delicate braid of sound in their shadows and the soft blue glow of
Pate's sign in the air.

And neither my young uncle across the room nor my mother
in the converted parlor across the hall nor my grandmother in her
bedroom—my grandfather's bed had been moved to the living
room—nor my father standing before the salvaged temple door
of his shack in the photograph beside my bed could tell me what
to make of it all. Nonetheless they were there around me, like the
trees, and while I would in the future find things that I could not
accept from them, I never had reason to doubt the motives or the
love behind anything they offered. When their lives are spread out
before me in the narrative that I have shaped to understand them
more clearly, the trees are there too, ceaseless in their parsing of
Pate's blue haze.

Our Hands in the History of It

When she wrung the necks of chickens for our Sunday meals, my grandmother summoned an uncommonly nimble articulation in her wrist that allowed her, after about three quick rotations of the bird, to cast it far enough from her to avoid spotting her apron with blood. It was a motion of the wrist that I don't remember in even the younger women of our family, nor in any of the men, including my father, gathered for our Sunday visits. But then again I've never seen anyone else wring the neck of a chicken, so what I guess I'm saying is that I can't imagine anyone even coming close to the smooth, articular motion that my grandmother introduced into her final rotation of the bird to send it in headless flight from her.

Usually she would have taken two pullets from the chicken yard and put them in a raised frame-and-wire coop for special feeding during the week before our visit. At some point in the past my grandfather had brought in some white leghorns to mix with the flock, but her choice for these special occasions continued to be her domineckers (dominiques), because the leghorns were too small to satisfy her protocol for a full serving on each plate—man's, woman's, or child's. Even if leghorns were allowed to grow beyond pullet size, for laying purposes, their eggs were not as good as the dominecker egg, she claimed. So it was the favored dominecker that she would take from the coop, gather under her arm, one hand over its neck and head, the other around its legs, and carry to the middle of the backyard. Releasing its legs and holding it by the head, she would rotate it quickly in the air by the weight of its body for as many turns as she judged the thickness of the neck to require. The image that I carry, half a century later, is of that particular motion—to say "flick" is to suggest too sharp and radical a motion—of her wrist in the conclusion, along with a casting away and a simultaneous stepping back while still in an almost graceful stoop, a half bow. The headless chicken, thrashing in the grass, is a blur to me and my cousins standing agape on the back porch or draped over one of the low limbs of the apple tree. We are waiting to watch her take the other dominecker from the coop and wring its neck.

The food and wine I remember and celebrate most fondly is that which I've been close to the source of. It's probably sentimental to think that these experiences actually are more intense and resonant the closer we are to the place of the sowing or gathering or preparation—and in the degree to which we have had a hand in any of this—but my own narratives of eating and drinking seem to favor that notion. The baker, dusty with flour, has just handed me a *bâtard* fresh from the oven, and I am eating it outside his shop. The Provençal village is bright with promise all around me. It is the best bread I have ever eaten. In another story it is a local wine and a train window in Tuscany letting onto the changing crosshatch of vineyard rows. My wife-to-be and I might think vaguely of the cheese and olives we have wrapped in wax paper, but for now there is nothing close in pleasure to this wine and the fleeing landscape of its origin. It's not that all of this is better than sex, but there are other passengers sharing our sleeping compartment. Also the nuns have a habit of looking into compartments, regardless of whether the curtains are open or drawn, in search of better seats and privacy.

O lost, and by the wind grieved, ghost thigh, drumstick, wishbone, come back again. The chicken that my grandmother is about to fry is going to be the best that I have ever eaten. As I said, these narratives of memory and celebration have for me an emotional ratio that relies on both the hands-on and the close-source quotients. My bread in Provence, even though I am at several removes from any chance at having a hand in its creation, is caught in the light of all its sources. Or at least I have romanticized it as such and that generates a nearly optimum prompt. Likewise the Tuscan wine, where the sense of source is even keener. It is late summer and the vines are heavy with grapes. The speed of the train accentuates the gradations of texture in the vineyards and gives the illusion of an actual winemaking already at work in the vines. As we pass through Chianti, the Gallo Nero (black rooster) logo of that region's wines flashes occasionally by our window, each image doubling and deepening the impression of those same roadside signs that we carry in memory from our recent drives into the countryside for lazy picnics among the olive groves or under the slender cypresses, all a part of the taste and texture of the soft wine and cheese and olives in brine and herbs, the fresh loaves of bread. We drink more of the wine and look out of the window now with the mild sadness of such departures.

I have my hands on the dominecker's scaly though surprisingly smooth legs and am carrying it to the black cast-iron pot under which my grandfather has a fire going. My grandmother will dip the headless chicken into the hot water to loosen its feathers and then let me or one of my cousins take it to the back porch while she is scalding the other one. We have spread newspapers for her. If she is not in too big a hurry she will let us help with the plucking. Everybody gets a tickle-feather to take home later, despite the fact that the air of the car will be tinctured with the odor of wet chicken. That odor, though, is nothing compared to the smell of the recently lit kerosene stove blending with the stench of burning pin feathers as my grandmother singes the plucked domineckers in the kitchen. She would normally dip them in melted paraffin to remove the pin feathers, but the store was out of stock. On the kitchen counter there is a blue and white paper carton of Humko Vegetable Shortening out of which she scoops a large portion of shortening for the hot skillet, and it's not until the butchered and dredged chicken is settled in this and popping, that the kitchen becomes a place my cousins and I want to spend any time in. My grandfather has butchered a hog recently and given her the lard he rendered, but she adds it to the melted shortening only sparingly and has never fried a chicken in it exclusively, as some of the neighbors do. Too greasy, she says. Throws the flavor off.

Proust may have written the book on this kind of thing, but his treatment of his Aunt Léonie's tea and *petites madeleines* is much too delicate and nuanced to handle the imprint that is forming in my brainpan now that the true frying has commenced in my grandmother's kitchen.

Don't misunderstand; it would suit me to do a lot less cooking than I do, and I'm sure my grandmother would have said the same for herself. If I were a boulevardier, I would be one with a proven weakness for good restaurants and cafés. If I were an especially rich boulevardier, I'd leave the boulevards once a week and jet to such places as the west coast of Ireland and be at Moran's of the Weir before the landing gear cooled, drinking one of their lighter draughts and eating salmon from the waters of history. This is not to say that I am backing down from my claim that the best food and drink for me is not only close-source but also a part of the work of my own hands. The family Moran's salmon, close to its source, is of the first order.

In the final reckoning, though, I cannot honor it in the way I honor the flounder that my friend Tom Huey and I caught and panfried in butter, dill weed, and lemon over an open fire on Cape Lookout one summer evening at sunset. One reason is that they were fresh out of the water. We had been drift-fishing in Lookout Bight and hooked them in the late afternoon after an otherwise luckless day, except for sighting some of the wild horses running along Shackleford Banks. In the slackness of the afternoon Tom kept mixing Cuba libres for us. By differing degrees our marriages were failing, and this was something I guess we thought we could do to stave off what was coming. Besides the Cuba libres, all we had for dinner was the flounder and half a loaf of Pepperidge Farm, which made the moment seem sort of scriptural and beatific.

When we woke the next morning and stumbled out of the tent, we found my Boston Whaler beached, dead weight on the sand with its heavy seaworthiness and an old forty-horse Evinrude that was about three times the weight of present models. We had neglected to factor in the low tide line in anchoring it, so there it was, thirty yards from the water, and we had to move it, foot by dark Bacardi foot, over the drying sand. All of that—the dead weight and sweat and near nausea, the beautiful emerald water we fished on, the recurring dread beneath the surface of our happiness, the wild horses, the fish finally taking our bait, the driftwood fire— is why it is the best flounder I have ever eaten. We had our hands in the history of it, and its provenance was all around us.

These stories of fish eaten fresh out of water—including those from sushi lovers—are implicitly competitive, and I give a high prize to a group of Asian tourists that a charter boat captain working out of St. Marks, Florida, told my group about. After boating a nice fish that one of the Asians had caught, the captain busied himself rigging an extra line and getting bait ready, only to look around and find the Asians sitting in a circle on the deck by the fish box. They had quit fishing, taken the fish out of the box, cut a strip from it, dipped it in a brown sauce, and were happily, ceremoniously, feasting. It was the best fish they had ever eaten.

I am going to the garden to pick collards after first frost. Even while tilling and working the compost into the ground and planting the small seeds, I knew the mature plants would take up too much space for the limited plot I had, but I wanted to feel the heft again in the harvesting and taste the taste I remember from country dinners. I plan to cook them for several hours with an unhealthy-sized piece of fatback in the pot. My boat is in the water and I am playing out line to troll along tide rips for blues. When they start striking we'll double back and try to cast without spooking them. The farm family, friends of my sister, calls to say come pick some Silver Queen; the tassels are turning. There are doves simmering in a broth of red wine, shallots, herbs, a little olive oil. Maybe a pinch of fennel. Even in a brief cataloging such as this, we begin to read our lives. My father is home on leave before shipping out for the Pacific. He has put on his red and black buffalo plaid shirt and is up in the pecan tree shaking a limb that we can't reach with the shaker pole. The pecans shower down on me. When I have filled another pail or two, we will take them inside and pick them, passing the nutcracker back and forth across the table as my mother gets ready to toast them with salt and butter. We will eat them fresh out of the oven early in the evening, and then tomorrow my father will go to war. My greatest fear, though, is that a limb will break or he will lose his purchase as he climbs higher. But he calls down to me and says to crack some of the pecans and make sure the lower ones aren't too green.

One Sunday we showed up at my grandparents' house un-announced. Maybe because the phones were out. I don't remem-ber. At any rate, my grandmother had not put any domineckers up for special feeding, and besides she said there weren't any really big enough to cook. We'd have to go with one of the leghorns. I don't think that this was a terribly unsettling event for her—the substitution of a leghorn—but I do think that our surprise visit and the need she felt to set a decent table for company, though not a two-chicken crowd, flustered her a bit. Still and all, she took her usual steady course to the chicken yard, singled out a shiny white leghorn, and began to work it toward a corner. This was a hot summer day in Mississippi, and the leghorn, smaller and more agile than her domineckers, tested her further, but she caught it and brought it to the middle of the yard to wring its neck.

Our Hands in the History of It

At the critical moment during the wringing, something apparently failed to engage in the small bones and musculature of her wrist, with the result that the chicken was not propelled as far from her as usual. In the bird's first wild flailing loop on the ground, several drops of blood from the neck stump came flying back at her and were absorbed in the white cotton of her apron. She was still wearing the apron that she had put on when we arrived. I can see her now, pulling the bib of the apron slightly away from her body and looking down at the stains on the cotton: three bright and neatly tailed meteors of red, seeming to be in a state of tension, still resisting their arrest in flight.

It was not a particularly dramatic mishap for her, though, as well as I can remember. She took note and went on with the work at hand. My grandfather later commented on the stains, but she explained it as a simple matter of not having cast the chicken far enough and then not being able to dodge the spattering of blood. The nuisance was in the prospect of having to wash and iron the apron again so soon. I am not making this out to be a badge for anything or a mark of my grandmother's mortality. It was a measure of her failing strength and facility of motion possibly, but she went on to wring the necks of scores of chickens and serve up the platters by which I continue to judge all fried chicken put before me.

After we ate the leghorn that day, along with buttered biscuits, mashed potatoes and gravy, pole beans, creamed corn, sliced tomatoes, pickled watermelon rind relish, iced tea, and fried peach pies, my grandfather and I walked to town to visit Mr. Woolfork's ice cream parlor, which we often did during my visits. The unusual thing, though to me it seemed providentially arranged and was a time-honored combination, was that Mr. Woolfork sold used pocket knives along with his ice cream. He kept them in cigar boxes under the counter and would bring them out if someone wanted to buy or trade knives.

A pocket knife was as essential as a shoe or a hat. My grandfather would whittle, lance a boil, cut an apple, or trim his toenails all with the same pocket knife. Mine was perhaps more a token knife, though I would find ways to use it in the woods, on fishing trips, and so on. I don't want to push the implications here, but our knives—their size, relative elaborateness—were a subject of comparison for me and my friends. But so too were our dogs, our bicycles, our new winter coats. For whatever meaning, they were fascinating objects—knives—and it was an enthralling event for me to walk into Mr. Woolfork's with my grandfather, order White House ice cream, and sort through the knives offered there for sale or trade. Probably my hope each time was that my grandfather would get me a different knife, but he did that only once during my entire childhood. As for his own knife, he would eventually wear down a blade and have to trade the knife and some money with Mr. Woolfork or go to the hardware store for a new one.

The strangeness of that union—ice cream and knives—did not register on me until much later, its force field of mystery as strong as ever. But that realization seemed only to deepen the mystery that I somehow sensed as a child: this particular hardware item in an ice cream parlor.

I call them the ice cream knives, and somehow I am trying to bring them to bear on the image of my grandmother and her ability to deal so summarily with her domineckers and leghorns. But the two images are bound to a time and a culture, and I have to leave them there in a loose and tentative circling. They seem to want to join in what might be a redefining of sacrament and sacrifice that I could understand—a liminal realm where there is a confluence of sacrifice, ritual, feasting, thanks giving—but it is a closure that I am finally incapable of forcing.

Besides, that would be asking too much of a motley assortment of used pocket knives in a cigar box, and also my grandmother would look back at me through the years, puzzled at such a far-fetched notion. At the moment she is looking down at me as I reach under the thin cloth she has spread over the leftovers on the table. There is not much fried chicken left except for a neck and a back with its vestigial tail pucker that she refers to as the preacher's nose. She knows I am full of White House ice cream but does not say anything. I am telling her about the ice cream knives. As I pick at the last of the nuggets of meat of the chicken's back, I look up at her and see that she still has on the apron. She looks down at the blood-stains and then back to me without any comment. I don't say anything either. I am eating the best chicken I have ever eaten.

Avian Voices

TRYING NOT TO KILL A MOCKINGBIRD

I made a deal with the deer: *I plant double, you take your half, I take my half.* They broke the deal before the ink was dry. Shoots of corn and beans, and later the flowers of peppers both hot and sweet—cayenne, tabasco, California Wonders—any tender offering, the deer went deep into my half. Even my heirloom zinnias. So I built a standard three-rail fence around the garden. Three rails, though, are like Tinkertoys to deer. They jumped my ridiculous fence and were back in the garden early the next morning, taking out a further swath of the promise of summer's bounty. I nailed iron posts to the fence corners for elevation and then strung plastic mesh fencing. They jumped into the mesh and, I think, immediately back out. The mesh apparently frightened them. I restrung it, and the garden became mine again. Until the mockingbird swooped down on me. I was transplanting Burpee's Big Boy tomato seedlings with a small shovel when he attacked, and I threw the shovel at him.

That was my first engagement with this, or any, mockingbird.

He pushed his claim to high office again when the Big Boy transplants had matured and were forming fruits. The least hint of red was his beacon. He would peck into the red just enough to ruin the entire tomato. And so I moved my tomato patch into an abandoned dog kennel fence and put the magic plastic mesh over the top to keep him off my Big Boys, Brandywines, German Johnsons, Black Krims, Mortgage Lifters, and Mr. Stripeys. This infuriated him, and he began to make dedicated swoops at me when I went out to get my morning newspaper.

According to the website Birdzilla, the mockingbird is very aggressive when it comes to defending its territory and nest, attacking even snakes, cats, and humans. The mockingbird is also a talented vocal mimic, Birdzilla tells us, and can imitate the sounds of many other birds, as well as manmade noises such as car alarms or squeaky pumps. I have read, too, that it can mimic the bark of a dog. Before federal laws were passed to protect native birds, so many mockingbirds were captured for the pet trade that they became scarce across much of their range.

This one is not scarce across any of my range of four acres. And it is clear from his derring-do and claim of dominion that he regards himself in heroic measures. Beowulf's windblown and birdlike ship comes to mind—here, in Seamus Heaney's translation:

> Over the waves, with the wind behind her
> and foam at her neck, she flew like a bird
> until her curved prow had covered the distance
> and on the following day, at the due hour,
> those seafarers sighted land,
> sunlit cliffs, sheer crags
> and looming headlands, the landfall they sought.

He is that very ship which has plied its way through difficult waters to reach sunlit cliffs, sheer crags, and looming headlands now transformed into my yard and vegetable garden. But he is outraged at the traditional gender assignment. The ship, a she. That's part of how I account for his animus. The other part is that he is just an asshole.

Among his other assumptions of regnancy, he has taken over my birdbath, which is a tidy copper basin designed for the feathered friends I have extended a welcome to: my Carolina wrens—*tea-kettle, tea-kettle, tea-kettle tea*, or sometimes simply *toodlewee*; the titmice—*Peter-Peter*; the goldfinches—*per-chick-o-ree* or *potato-chips*, also *zwe-zeeeee*; and my favorite, the common sparrow—*come-come-where-where-all-together-down-the-hill*. (Voices rendered by the Audubon Society *Field Guide to North American Birds*.) In their bathing, these favored birds of mine have a delicate economy of motion, soft flicks and twitches, conserving water as if they know others are waiting in line. The mockingbird's bath is an orgy of thrashing and writhing about. When he has finished, one of the innocents alights on the rim of the basin and looks with disbelief at the thimble of water remaining.

And so daintiness and restraint are not qualities inscribed in the mockingbird psyche. Nor is reason. Mockingbirds will attack their reflection in a window, hubcap, or mirror, often with such intensity that they injure or kill themselves. My mockingbird went at himself for hours in the side-view mirror of my Ford Ranger pickup, repeatedly challenging the invader with what the Audubon guide describes as a harsh *chack*. (To be fair, the bird is capable of music, but is it finally his? The songs of thirty-six other species were recognized from the recording of one mockingbird in Massachusetts. Serious personality disorder there, or unrelenting guile.)

As for injury and death in general, those losses are part of the natural order of a bird's life. Usually it is death from above. Have you ever seen a bird's eyes not constantly parsing the sky? Landward there are cats ready to pounce. And other threats you wouldn't dream. A black snake climbed a column on my front porch and ate the eggs in a nest my sparrows had built on the overhead beam. The natural order, I figured. Not that I was not chilled to see the snake on the beam above me, its overlapping coil gleaming ebony in the morning light. I poked it down with a rake and took it to a

Avian Voices

thick winter-honeysuckle bush at the edge of my yard. I wanted to keep it around to eat the field mice and rats that had my garage in mind. The bulge of three sparrow eggs in the snake's body was unmistakable.

Other sparrows had a nest nearby in the bend of a downspout just outside one of my front windows. The nest was at eye level with the window, and I would stand there to watch the mother bird feed her four peeps. On the day after I delivered the black snake to its safe haven, I looked out to find the nest empty. On the ground by the downspout were the dead bodies of two of the peeps. These were not fledglings, and I reasoned that the black snake had come from the winter-honeysuckle and had its fill of the two other baby sparrows in the nest and then dropped these two to the ground. Or they attempted flight.

So it goes. The snares and foils are many. Birds mistake the large windows on either side of my house for open passages and fly into them. I can hear their bonks as they hit the glass. I go out and try to help them get reoriented. A gorgeous yellow-shafted flicker wobbled around for twenty minutes or so after I gave it a gentle massage, and then it took flight into the trees bordering my creek. Doves hit particularly hard; they are fleet and sometimes don't recover from the collision with what looks like to them *plein air*. One afternoon I heard an unusually forceful hit and went out to find a dead dove on the grass. I plucked the feathers, freed the breast, and took it inside. Sautéed in butter with a sliver of garlic and hint of thyme, it was three-star Michelin, four-toque Gault Millau.

More recently a pine siskin collided with a window. As with the dove, I was unable to revive it. It reminded me, though, of the ortolan, a bunting that some French gourmands drown in Armagnac, pluck, roast, and eat whole. I couldn't bring myself to eat the little pine siskin, not even if prepared in the manner of my dove. As for the ortolan, European Union member states have banned the deliberate killing or capture of these birds because of their endangered status. The French have been lax in enforcing the ban, and poachers continue to trap this sparrow-sized bird. Diners cover their faces with linen napkins and eat the entire bird, though the less venturesome forgo the head, beak, and feet. The covering of the face is said to have been initiated by a priest (friend to French gourmand Jean Anthelme Brillat-Savarin), who did so to hide his gluttony from God.

I have followed a red-shouldered hawk—*kee-yeeear*—from the time he was a fledgling. He was in a black walnut tree at the border of my property when I first spotted him, and for the past few years I have watched through binoculars as he drops down precipitously on field mice. He will also eat grubs. And occasionally I find clusters of fluffy gray feathers in the grass, but I do not know if he or some other raptor has intercepted a flying dove. That would be no small feat. My mockingbird will attack other birds, and me, but he does not mess with this hawk. I was elated recently to spot my hawk and a female, only just arrived, resting together on a piece of sculpture in my back yard. I am hoping for young red-shoulders soon from their pairing.

In my mind the sculpture creates a kind of liminal space, a threshold where particular birds cross over and meet me in a realm otherwise unavailable to me or them. A fanciful notion, I know, but in myth we are forever joined with the avian. Often the wax of our wings fails us, and we plunge. Other times we soar.

My sculpture appropriates an iron wheel rim from an old farm wagon. Welded within the circle of that rim is a sinuous *S* of metal, making for a yin-yang effect inside the circle. Bluebirds often perch on the sculpture, though always solo for some reason. The smaller birds tend not to perch there, perhaps because the wheel rim is too wide to afford a secure purchase. Or the mojo of the mandala is too much for them. I don't know. I am not a birder by any stretch, but I can sit and watch these creatures—in the bird bath or on the wheel rim or in flight—for long periods of time, rapt with fascination and wonder.

In all of this behavior, I detect a manifest social order in the bird kingdom, and I don't mean simply a pecking order. The cowbird, for instance, is a brood parasite. It lays its eggs in the nests of songbirds. Some of them will reject the cowbird egg; others will lay down a new nest lining over it. But most will rear the young cowbird, which matures quickly at the expense of the host's young, pushing them out of the nest or taking their food. Added to this parasitic behavior is the cowbird's lack of any prepossessing physical attractiveness, at least to my eye. I watched a brown-headed cowbird alight near three of my common sparrows on a section of fence. Sort of like Charlie Chaplin disciples, the sparrows edged away in a comical sideways avoidance maneuver. The cowbird tip-toed awkwardly along the fence railing after them, trying to seem nonchalant but making an obvious bid to be a buddy. He edged over, they twiddled a few steps away, he edged over again, and the sparrows finally took flight. The cowbird remained there, alone and gripping the fence rail in ignominy.

I am not going to kill the mockingbird. Truth to tell, I have become amused at his antics. Yesterday morning I walked out toward my garden and he took flight from the fence. I have a screen-house that is elevated on wood pilings, but there is only a three-foot space between its floor beam and the ground. The mockingbird made a straight course for that restricted opening and flew under the screenhouse and out the other side. Show-off. But maybe a hint of détente. He didn't swoop down on me.

In *To Kill a Mockingbird* Miss Maudie Atkinson tells Scout that "mockingbirds don't do one thing but make music for us to enjoy. They don't eat up people's gardens, don't nest in corncribs, they don't do one thing but sing their hearts out for us. That's why it's a sin to kill a mockingbird."

Up against Miss Maudie's sentimentality—and my own in tracing the delights of my little birds—is an alternative. In the closing scene of David Lynch's *Blue Velvet*, there is a robin on a tree branch. The robin is central to a dream that Laura Dern's character has had, and she interprets its return as the return of love. The scene is controversial, but I regard it as ironic. The robin (which, by the way, is a stuffed robin) has a bug in its beak, and its gaze registers nothing resembling love. Dern's character is in denial of the reality of predation, dramatized in chilling detail by Dennis Hopper's character as he inhales whatever it is, helium or nitrous oxide, from a face mask and enters a deeper chamber of his psychosis. And so what are the truths that birds bring to us in their perches and flights, and in our dreams of them?

In the Venerable Bede's *Historia ecclesiastica gentis Anglorum* (circa 731 AD), we are told of a bird who flew into a festive hall from the night of rain and snow outside, only to pass into that night again through a window on the other side of the hall. Such is our brief passage through life. It is from darkness into darkness, unknown on either side. But there is the warmth and light and joy and sadness of the hall. In my imagination it is a mead hall, with venison and pheasant, quail, the pig on the spit, dogs asleep by the ancestral fire, bold women and men our friends, laughter, song, weeping over spoken poems of human error and downfall. We are that bird in flight. But we are not alone. Flying with us are the wrens and titmice, the goldfinches, my two hawks, the common sparrows. *Come! Come! Where? Where? All Together Down the Hill!*

Snugfit Eye Patch

THE MONOCULAR PROOF

Othello to Iago on Desdemona's handkerchief:
. . . give me the ocular proof . . .
Make me to see't. . . .

OTHELLO, ACT III

When I arrived home following a weekend camping trip, my mother's welcoming smile vanished in a look of concern, and she told me that my eye was crossed. She meant my artificial eye. I had lost my right eye the year before, at age twelve, while visiting my grandparents. A rock flew up from the open chute of a lawn mower. "Got it knocked out," as my male friends described it. Looking in the mirror after my mother informed me of the canted eye, I saw that the prosthesis was pointed outward, suggesting both quandary and alertness toward that side of the world to which I was blind.

What had happened was that on the camping trip I had wiped the sleep from that eye and in the process had turned it in its socket. Having only the small creek beside our tent as a source of reflection, I did not know the eye was turned. Nor did my fellow Boy Scout campers tell me. Perhaps they were sparing me embarrassment. Maybe the eye awoke in them a kindness, which we normally were awkward with. There was the possibility also that they considered the eye off limits, taboo.

One of the mothers fetched us from the rendezvous point of our camping trip to drive us home. Seated beside me in the back seat of the car was the mother's daughter Martha, along for the ride. I had a crush on her, though not one that I had announced—or fully understood. She had on shorts, and there were hairs on top of her thighs, barely pubescent. A film of perspiration glistened lightly above her upper lip. The nearness of all that—Martha herself, her bare legs, the delicate hair, the film of perspiration—set off stirrings of attraction I had not known before. She did not mention my crossed eye, nor afterward did she ever greet me with anything other than a conventional cheeriness.

That experience on the camping trip and with Martha in the back seat, and its various iterations—insecurity with girls when I was young, embarrassment at compromised depth perception, assignment to a vague status of being different, and so on—led to my decision to give up the fake eye and wear an eye patch. A kind of transformation. There is hyperbole in that notion, but I cannot overstate the degree of my sensitivity, my self-consciousness, in the face of what seemed to me an attention—implacable at times, subtle at best—focused on the motionless eye. And the feeling that half of my countenance, that which the eye gave back to the world, was misleading and insufficient. You could question the logic of my decision and suggest that a patch invites even more attention. True, but the patch presents a decidedly different and, for me, more comfortable visage than I could find otherwise. There is also the fact that logic had little or no governance in a mind vexed by memories of embarrassments, represented early on by the image I had formed of my crossed eye fixed on the periphery of the campsite as though searching for what friends alongside the creek were seeing straight on. And of Martha in the back seat.

And so, years later, when I entered graduate school, where I knew not a soul, I sewed an elastic band on a crude black patch, bound it around my head, opened the dormitory door, and presented my transformed and openly monocular self to the world. In the walk to my classroom, I had the feeling, new to me, both of freedom and utter uncertainty. Mine was nothing like, say, a war wound, though I can empathize with the veteran strapping on a prosthetic arm or leg for the first time and walking out of the clinic. Part of that long walk is in accepting that people notice but hoping that the agency of substitution and one's adjusted identity will in time render their gaze neutral, harmless.

All of this, at graduate school and later at home, was in the mid-1960s, and there was no internet to search for suppliers of eye patches. I inquired of an optometrist regarding possible sources, and he gave me the address of a supplier in California, Snugfit Eye Patch Company. I ordered a trial patch. It was far superior to the patches one finds in the eye section of the first aid shelf of drugstores. In fact, so keen was my anxiety over the possibility of ever having to go back to that shelf, I ordered a lifetime supply of black eye patches from Snugfit. Two boxes full, a single box now remaining, yellowed with age. It features as illustration an attractive woman with the Snugfit eye patch. She is coifed in a 1940s hair-do. Which would seem to compromise the breakaway gender spin they have put on things—avoiding any hint of male stereotypes such as the suave be-patched Hathaway Man in the shirt ads of the mid-twentieth century. But she is smiling, an open summons to our gaze, and that assurance and candor continue to set off a ripple of bonhomie in me, the target audience.

So far as I can determine, the Snugfit Eye Patch Company no longer exists. They were in Yucaipa, California. The post office box is listed on a small label that has been pasted over a former address. There is a Snugfit Eye Patch Company currently listed online, but the Yucaipa Chamber of Commerce has no entry for it. There is yet another Snugfit Eye Patch Company listed online for Green Bay, Wisconsin. Not that I plan to order any more eye patches, but out of curiosity I called the phone number. It was no longer in service. The great Snugfit mystery.

There are ample sources, though, if you need an eye patch. As for selection, you can get a hot pink eye patch, a hot pink camo eye patch, or a standard army camo eye patch. Also an American flag eye patch. One company offers a cryptic two-pack, a red wagon on one patch, a yellow backhoe on the other. And there is a black eye patch that, in the spirit of Halloween, carries a skull and cross-bones. All of which is to say that I am not alone in having sought out a patch for my needs.

My graduate school days coincided with the escalation of American troops in Vietnam. In 1965 the draft call was the highest since the Korean War. In that same year I received notice from the Selective Service System that my student status exempted me from the draft and my classification had been changed to II-S, exemption as a student.

The story of my various classifications over the years is a convoluted one. Following my registration with the Selective Service System in 1957, I was classified IV-F, owing to the loss of my eye, and not qualified for military service. I wrote my local Selective Service board with a petition not to be classified IV-F.

My father had served in the First Marine Division in World War II, surviving both the Peleliu and Okinawa invasions. One of his fellow platoon members later informed me that his division received a Presidential Unit Citation for each of those battles. My father did not bring his medals or citations home, nor when I was young did he ever talk to me of his war experiences. I had always had an awareness of the dangers he faced and survived, and I realize now that in writing my letter of appeal in 1957 for classification other than IV-F, well before I knew of the Presidential Unit Citations, I was guided by the sense that I needed to take his example of service as a model.

My letter, though, was a model of the sophomoric. I had a sense of duty to country, but the letter was informed mainly by my father's influence in my life. Not that our relationship was always one of harmony, nor am I any kind of superpatriot. Incidentally, in seeming contradiction to my earlier request for military service qualification, I marched against the Vietnam War in 1970.

None of the latter sentiment against war figured in my letter of petition for revocation of the IV-F classification in 1957. I laid out my bona fides with a zeal that is unavailable to me today, yet heartening in its testimony to the ingenuousness and at the same time passion of intent that one can call forth as a youth. I opened my bid with the insistence that the A which I had earned in the wrestling portion of a physical education course was incontestable proof of my fitness for the demands of military service. Next I listed the high school sports I had participated in, with attention to the medals won in track and field. I listed Boy Scout merit badges and camping expeditions. As for leadership potential, I was student body president in high school, Best All Around in the superlatives vote. The list goes on. I ended up with a I-Y, not a IV-F, meaning I was thus qualified for service in a national emergency or time of war.

Though there were many citizens during World War II with legitimate reasons for a IV-F classification, it nonetheless carried a stigma, and the term "draft dodger" came to be associated with the IV-F classification. Even at a young age I was aware of this negative characterization. And when I opened that first letter from the local board of the Selective Service System, I felt the full burn of that stigma.

The clerk who signed my notification card was our next-door neighbor, and I was dating her daughter off and on, with hopes for more on. Her daughter knew of my eye, but the card her mother signed, which was apparently discussed in their household, became a kind of quarantine placard. No chilliness on her part, certainly no animus, but a halt to any romantic progress. Palimpsest of the half-forced cheeriness that Martha beamed at me in school hallways following my backseat sideshow after the camping trip.

This accounting of my father's military service and my efforts to get my classification changed goes to a truth about one's sense of manhood, a truth not limited to my own generation: that one is somehow inadequate, incomplete, less a man, when one loses a part of the body, whether a limb, an eye, or a loss that results in disfigurement. (I am sure there are equivalent forces shaping a young female's sense of womanhood, but that is outside my focus here.)

This can be particularly acute in one's need for a father's approval. Or one's perception of how he fulfills or fails his father's expectations. My own father spent his whole life striving to fit the image of manhood—work hard, show no emotion, be brave, be proud, man up—that his father put before him. And that my father in turn put before me—vocally, and by example. For instance, I have a letter to my father's platoon members from a man, Jack "Tex" Price, who visited my father after the war: *I reminded him how tough he was on us, but also told him I appreciated it. He helped most of us get back, where some would not, had he not been around.*

I wanted to be like my father. But after the loss of my eye, I sensed that my father's attitude toward me shifted, that he no longer saw me as a son who would be able to fit his concept of manliness. Not that he was cruel or remonstrative, just that he did not seem to look on me in the same manner as before my loss. He was protective of me, though, perhaps to a fault. He wanted to keep me out of further harm's way. My mother was protective of me also, but her faith in me remained steadfast.

It was not until my teenage years that my father, perhaps at my mother's urging, began to include me in more of his activities—fishing, going out at night to farm ponds with our carbide lamps atop our heads to gig frogs, dressing the legs out for my mother to fry, teaching me to drive our Chevrolet Bel Air. Not only did he have to reach over and help me turn corners, I consistently stalled the car when I let out the clutch. It was during this time that we moved to South Florida, and instead of continuing with the Bel Air, he put me on a bulldozer and turned me loose on a vast open field where he was supervisor of development for farmland. Not much chance of crashing into anything, and a simple clutch maneuver. It was then that his attitude toward me shifted more to one of approval. I would take the bulldozer out with Desmond, the Bahamian, and we would work all day bulldozing brush, pushing it into a pile, dousing it with a mix of gasoline and diesel fuel, and setting it aflame. Woosh. Work. No thought of being one-eyed.

Sometimes on weekends my father and I would drive from our home in Pahokee to Port Salerno to fish with our neighbor Bill Jones on his thirty-foot powerboat *Vergie*. Well out of sight of land, and with no sonar fish-finder, we dropped cut bait into the depths of the Atlantic and hoped we were over fish. Usually we had a good catch of grouper and red snapper to take home. I was not invited every Sunday they went out, and when I was invited I usually got seasick. My father, meaning well, would give me saltines and send me below to a bunk, not realizing that the diesel fumes in the small cabin added to my wretchedness. All the while my father was on the deck above, pulling in fish, whooping and hollering with Bill Jones, drinking beer—free of the savagery and ash of war that he had emerged from, unscathed except for a piece of shrapnel that he still carried.

My father's exuberance on the deck above and at other times on the water informs my fishing today. But there are challenges with monocular vision that I find more pronounced as I age. Owing to the lack of sight on one side, I am hampered in my casting with both fly rod and spinning rig, fearful of hooking the angler next to me, especially in the tight space of a drift boat. Or in any boat where two or three anglers are lined up casting into the same space of water. At times I have requested the outside position, with no angler on my blind side. One of my pals half-jokingly says I am trying to play the one-eyed card. Sometimes he yields, sometimes not. We banter back and forth. My friends, all in all, take me pretty much as I present myself, and the subject of my vision rarely comes up. And when it does, the tenor is usually ironic or that of playful humor. Which is fine by me.

One thing that confounds me, though, is when a stranger, outright or early on in the conversation, brings up my patch or wants to know what happened to my eye. I am civil, but brief, in my response. Typically I ask if a family member or friend has a similar condition, is that why they have inquired? Almost without fail I know immediately that any potential for further relationship with that person is less than zero. A notable exception is the time a man standing in front of me in a waiting line at the Barcelona airport turned and asked about my eye. Before I could give my customary reply, he hastened to explain that he was an ophthalmologist and had a particular interest in monocular vision. A boarding line in Barcelona. An ophthalmologist. With an interest in monocular vision. ¡Dios mío!

Ruskin tells us, "The greatest thing a human soul ever does in this world is to *see* something, and tell what it *saw* in a plain way." This speaks to the primacy of vision among the senses. If Othello can *see* the handkerchief, have the ocular proof, he will know Desdemona has been untrue. Or so Iago would have him believe. Shakespeare puts a spin on the notion of vision and its privilege in our sense of the world when Lear beseeches blind Gloucester on the storm-ravaged heath:

> O, ho, are you there with me? No eyes in your head.
> . . . Yet you see how this world goes.

To which Gloucester replies:

> I see it feelingly.

It would be dumb and ungracious of me to try to appropriate Shakespeare's trope of seeing, understanding how the world goes. In full blindness. *I see it feelingly.* Nor would I try to halve the trope—half-feelingly. Best to say, I see it differently. Snugly fitted.

You Dumb Bell

The greeting on the face of the valentine, *You Dumb Bell*, says more about my mother than about the recipient—my father, the putative "dumb bell" in question. The valentine is in the shape of a dumb-bell, the weight used for exercise and made popular during the time my mother gave the valentine to my father, the early 1930s, before they married. When opened, the little dumbbell carries the jussive *Get Onto the Fact That I'd Like to Be Your Valentine*. Above that directive float two hearts, a single arrow piercing them both.

My father, though, needed little assurance that Lucie Belle Page was his valentine. Already during their closely supervised courtship he had lifted his cigarette—remember, no romantic movie of that era lacked a cigarette—and spelled out "I love you" in the air of the Page living room in Como, Mississippi. They were not allowed to sit together on the settee during his visits. My mother's older brother, Damon, a Puritan of the first water, was in the adjacent room, alert to any threat to his notion of purity. You will recall the Puritans who interrupted the nuptial party in Hawthorne's "The May-Pole of Merry Mount." They shot the dancing bear and cropped the locks of the bridegroom who had danced with and then wed the Lady of the May. Breaks your heart. Puritans bent on killing any merriment. Damon would have been in their front ranks.

When I say that the valentine reveals more about my mother's sensibility than my father's, I do not mean that he was without a sense of levity, as evidenced in his amorous smoke signal sent across the room in secret. But my mother had an impulsiveness and whimsy that he lacked. I have a photograph of her around age seventeen in a neighbor's lily pond. She wears a one-piece bathing suit of black wool jersey, and she is standing among the lily pads with one hand on the concrete lip of the small pond. The waterline is at her breasts, and white lily blossoms surround her. She is smiling, as if to say, "Look at me now. I've snuck out and jumped into Vashti Lewis's lily pond. And Damon can't do anything about it."

My father, on the other hand, while capable of the "I love you" sent in wisps of smoke, would sit and talk of Caterpillar bulldozers or recite to her the mnemonic "Washington and Jefferson Made Many a Joke." w-a-j-m-m-a-j: Washington, Adams, Jefferson, Madison, Monroe, Adams, Jackson. "Van Buren Had to Pay, Taylor's Frying Pan Broke. Lincoln Just Gasped, 'Heaven Guard America!'" He could take it all the way to FDR, who was president at the time.

The Depression did not need a Wall Street crash to enter the Deep South. Hard times had been a way of life for most people in the South forever, and FDR's New Deal, while a grand effort and a success, by and large, had a limited effect in some areas. My mother's family in Mississippi played the economic hand they were dealt with remarkable skill and decidedness. They tended a large vegetable garden in season, cultivated pecan and fruit trees, raised chickens, and had cows for milk, cream, and butter.

Butter was on the table every day. My mother did the churning. She was instructed by her mother, though, never to straddle the churn. That would be vulgar. The churning was to be done side-saddle, so to speak. But when her mother left the room, my mother straddled the churn, pumping the dasher like a wanton, intent on getting the butter to the top as soon as possible. To churn to the side, her body twisted, was much more physically demanding. And slower. There were lily ponds out there waiting to be jumped into.

And there was sweet sorghum cane to be had for peeling and chewing. My mother's father had a sorghum field and a small mill for making sorghum syrup—imagine an earthy, mild caramel flavor—which was put up in jars for the winter cupboard. His mule Thunder, named for unceasing flatulence, was harnessed to a long pole attached to the sorghum mill. Thunder plodded in a circle to put in motion the gears that governed the crushing mechanism. Sorghum cane was fed into the mill, and the juice that flowed from it was soon in the settling tank and then into copper pans for stirring and evaporation over the wood fire until it arrived at proper consistency.

My mother went one day to the field to fetch canes of sorghum for her and her siblings. Thunder was given a rest, and my mother's father collected choice stalks for her to deliver to the house. There Damon would cut the cane into sections and apportion them to his siblings.

As she made her way up the dirt road through the field, my mother stopped and put one of the canes beneath her heel. She didn't have a knife, but she was determined to get into the sweetness of the sorghum before her brother had a chance to use it as demand for payment on indulgences from his papacy. As she pulled up on one end of the cane, the section beneath her heel split, forming a razor-sharp edge along both sides of the separation. When she released the end of the cane, it sought its natural bind and caught a portion of flesh in its vise, cutting deeply into her heel. My mother began hopping around and kicking to free herself. When liberated from the cane, her heel was bleeding profusely into the dust of the road.

Perhaps as a reaction to the trauma—or perhaps just coincidence, the cut and a natural onset—her menses began. Blood trickled down her thighs and joined that issuing from the cut in her heel. She did not know which was which in the confluence that soaked into the dust, nor did she know what was wound and what was not. But the dust helped stanch the flow from her heel, and she gathered herself for the delivery of the sweet cane to the house. There in a bedroom her mother explained to her what one realm of her life was now given over to.

I never knew of any of this until, in her late years, my mother showed me the scar on her heel and told me of its source. Though she did not provide all of the details in my narrative, I summon them to make her story more vivid and at the same time mysterious and elusive to me. I do not want her generic or sentimentalized. I want her to be somewhere between the girl surrounded by white blossoms in a lily pond and the young woman bleeding in the cane field with a lone scar in the making and her womb opened to the world. I want her also in fixed defiance of her brother Damon and what he stands for.

That is not to say that Damon was an evil person. In adulthood he was a hardworking man, decent enough. But he retained the rigidity and intense censoriousness of his earlier years. When my mother's mother had her sixth and final child, Joe David Page, Damon left the house in a fury and moved into the barn. He told his parents that they could barely feed the children they had and now they were bringing another mouth to the table. I can find empathy for him, however, in the humiliation he suffered at the hands of a man who sold him a baby coffin when he was a young boy. Damon passed by the hardware store in town and saw in the window what he took to be a little boat. He wanted to float in the little boat past the bluffs on the river nearby. He saved his money and took it to the man, who assured him that he could float past the bluffs in it. When Damon brought his little boat home, his father told him it was a baby coffin.

It's possible also that I can find feeling for him in his marriage. He married a woman, Jennie Ruth Hay, who had just been married for two days to a Mr. Sweat from Arkansas. (I am told that she was particularly insistent that her family pronounce his last name properly: "Sweet.") After her one-night honeymoon, she returned to her parents' home, and the next morning Mr. Sweat had left her trousseau luggage on the front porch. Soon after that, Jennie Ruth married Damon. She was the bane of our Sunday visits to their home, especially with her unrelenting reminders that she was a member of the Daughters of the American Revolution. Nothing we could do or say escaped her judgment. My mother despised her but instructed my sisters and me to mind our manners. At some point before Jennie Ruth died, she stipulated that there be no birth date on her gravestone, only the year of her death. Vain into eternity, she waited there to be joined by the finally hapless Damon. In the months before his death he claimed that the nurses at the assisted care center were "having their way" with him. When my sisters were clearing out his house to settle his estate, they discovered *Playboy* magazines in his closet. I'm confident that he found more release there than any he found with the one-night honeymooner Jennie Ruth.

I was living in the South of France in 1990 when word came from my sisters in Mississippi that they had taken my mother to the hospital in Memphis. Given the cost of last-minute transatlantic airfares, they suggested that I remain in France until they could advise me further about her condition. After their call, I went to a restaurant near Place Masséna in Nice called Spaghettisimo or some such. I've Googled and Binged for current restaurants there but cannot find a Spaghettisimo. I wanted to verify its name so as to re-create in sum that fraught moment in my life. I recall distinctly the uncertainty, the dread of guilt should I not go to my mother in an hour of need, the vacancy that I would feel if she died while I was in France.

When I had finished my pasta, I walked to a promontory overlooking the Mediterranean. The sun was behind a bank of clouds. As I looked into the sky, the sun broke from the clouds and cast a soft brilliance across the surface of the sea and spilled onto the city. It was a gift of light from my mother. Lucie, *lux*, light. *I am okay*, she said, *go back and have some espresso. Stay there until I need you. I've survived Damon, open bleeding in a sorghum cane field, and, who knows, possible drowning in a lily pond.*

The last words my mother spoke to me were, "You feel warm." It was 1992, two years after the sun broke from the clouds over the water and brought my mother across the ocean to me. She was in the hospital in Memphis again, and she would die there, but I did not know that. My sisters assured me that they would watch over her and get her home when she recovered. I had to get back to my work in North Carolina. I leaned over to hug and kiss my mother good-bye, and she commented on my warmth. "You feel warm." What she meant was that I felt as though I had a fever and she needed to get up and tend to me. Put a flannel cloth with Vicks VapoRub on my chest. Read *The Adventures of Tom Sawyer* out loud. Fix me some cream of tomato soup and a grilled cheese sandwich. Tell me Little Moron jokes and why the chicken crossed the road. To get to the other side.

Ah, Lucie, you dumb bell.

Where Books Fall Open

Some thirty or forty linear feet of my poetry library played a minor role in the movie *The Portrait*, starring Lauren Bacall and Gregory Peck. A minor role in a minor movie. It was directed by Arthur Penn, but it is no *Bonnie and Clyde* by any tally. That saddens me, as I was a Penn fan and I had a pleasant talk with him on the movie set, mainly about our mutual friend, the poet Richard Wilbur.

I say linear feet because that is apparently the metric by which prop managers deal with books. Once they hear that you have books and determine that those books have the right look for the movie, they negotiate to rent enough of them to fill the designated shelf space. A few linear feet of my poetry books made the final cut in one scene, and a linear inch appears in Peck's hand as he descends the stairs in another scene. He tells Bacall that he has found a misplaced car insurance policy tucked away in a book of Richard Wilbur's poems.

Aware myself that things get misplaced in the world, I had inventoried my books before sending them out to bear witness for literature—and bring home revenue for additional books for my shelves.

A book of Whittier's poems, nicely bound, the pages gilt-edged, did not make it back home. I cannot say that I felt this loss keenly—in the way, say, I would feel the loss of a book inscribed to me by a fellow writer—because Whittier is not one of my favorite poets. Some of his poems have historical value for me, and I've always liked the sound and incremental syllable-spread of his name. John Greenleaf Whittier. What the ancient rhetoricians called a rhopalic. *Friends, Romans, countrymen*. But Whittier's sentimentality has kept him generally unvisited on my bookshelf.

Nonetheless I did feel the loss of the book, owing to the fond memory I have of my initial engagement with the physical book itself—and to the situational irony of that experience. I bought it in a used book store in Kitty Hawk on the Outer Banks of North Carolina during a summer vacation. When I took the book from the shelf and tested its heft, it fell open to "Snow-Bound." Standing there beneath a ceiling fan that barely stirred the humid coastal air in the room, I skimmed Whittier's once-famous *winter idyl*. The poem renders in nostalgic measures a family's experiences during a winter storm that raged for three days in rural Massachusetts when the poet was a boy.

You will recall, or your grandparents will recall, that the snowbound poet and his family are drawn into even closer intimacy as they face *the chill embargo of the snow*. They go about their evening chores—bringing in firewood, littering the stalls with hay, feeding the livestock—and then they gather around the hearth-fire to share stories. There is no question but that these storytellers have a snug relationship with the "Angel of the backward look." Nostalgia reigns.

Closing the book and holding its spine in my palm, I could see along the length of its fore-edge a thin line of discoloration and wear that marked the location of "Snow-Bound." Pilgrims, tourists, whoever under whatever banner, they had collectively worn a path to the same place at the altar rail.

This set me to thinking of books that I have returned to over the years and how any one of them could also be expected to fall open, as did the Whittier, to a favored passage or poem or story. Likely many of your own books would fall open in some of the same places:

> Lend me a looking-glass;
> If that her breath will mist or stain the stone,
> Why, then she lives. [But Cordelia is of course "dead
> as earth."]

> There's a certain Slant of light,
> Winter Afternoons—
> That oppresses, like the Heft
> Of Cathedral Tunes—

> Heavenly Hurt, it gives us—
> We can find no scar,
> But internal difference—
> Where the Meanings, are—

> None may teach it—Any—

I was a Flower of the mountain yes when I put the rose in my hair like the Andalusian girls used or shall I wear a red yes and how he kissed me under the Moorish wall and I thought well as well him as another and then I asked him with my eyes to ask again yes and then he asked me would I yes to say yes my mountain flower and first I put my arms around him yes and drew him down to me so he could feel my breasts all perfume yes and his heart was going like mad and yes I said yes I will Yes.

There were many words that you could not stand to hear and finally only the names of places had dignity. Certain numbers were the same way and certain dates and these with the names of the places were all you could say and have them mean anything. Abstract words such as glory, honor, courage, or hallow were obscene beside the concrete names of villages, the numbers of roads, the names of rivers, the numbers of regiments and the dates.

Proust's tea and madeleines; Odysseus's homecoming, he in disguise and his dog Argos's tail thumping in recognition before breathing his last; Achilles's shield; Auden's take on the implications of that shield,

> That girls are raped, that two boys knife a third,
> Were axioms to him, who'd never heard
> Of any world where promises are kept,
> Or one could weep because another wept.

Eudora Welty's "The Petrified Man," her character who asks, "Funny ha-ha or funny peculiar?" How Milton's serpent approaches Eve "with tract oblique." The cunning of indirection. On and on, books falling open, the canon ever changing, each register inevitably of the reader's time and place.

Mine was not a bookish family, though I could count on a new Hardy Boys mystery every year under the Christmas tree. And I cherished the slipcase edition of *The Adventures of Tom Sawyer* that my Uncle Jack sent me from Marshall Field's in Chicago. In search of more such adventures, I became a regular at our town library, which was housed in a sweet little church that the local Episcopalians had outgrown and given to the town. And so my engagement with books came to be informed by the light that transfused softly through the body of the Virgin Mary, the Dove of Peace descending upon her in Annunciation, Christ in Gethsemane, *O my Father, if it be possible, let this cup pass from me.* Christ laboring to Golgotha, *He bearing his cross went forth unto the place of the skull.*

Where Books Fall Open

The Resurrection, *O death where is thy sting? O grave where is thy victory?* All in the stained glass of the windows surrounding me.

As I was innocent of the concepts of faith and salvation beyond mere rote, those stained glass representations had only a nominal claim on my mind. But the lucency, the transformed quality of the light itself, coming through the windows made for a sense of magic and the ineffable. Sitting at my library table, surely I must have sensed that the light falling on the book before me was enhanced by its union with mystery and miracle, though I could not have given voice to any such notion.

In my hunger for adventure I typically gravitated to the table beneath Shadrach, Meshach, and Abednego. With Nebuchadnezzar's fiery furnace behind them, they were in league with the Hardy Boys and dangers evaded, whether providential or by Boy Scout preparedness. The library tables themselves, and the chairs complementing them, came out of the furnace of World War II. They had been made by soldiers of Rommel's Afrikakorps interned in a POW camp, Camp Como, in my home county in Mississippi. Some of the prisoners were put to work in the cotton fields. Others made the clunky tables and chairs which I now realize were simulacra of taverns in the Bavaria of their wistful dreams.

In addition to the name of the deft and relentless Rommel in my mind was the name of Isabel Lamb. Isabel lived in my hometown and had worked in the canteen of the POW camp. She began an affair with one of the German soldiers, a former Panzer tank driver. You would think that she would have taken up with one of Rommel's officers, given that they had less supervision and thus more opportunity for an assignation, but instead she found romance with a tank driver who was assigned to a Singer sewing machine in the camp. He repaired uniforms, let out pants, and such. He was reassigned to a camp in Idaho, digging potatoes, beets, and onions. Isabel was heartbroken and became known in town as one who "had been up there at Como fucking Nazis."

And so I sat in my chair under the silent furnace of Nebuchadnezzar, a book open before me on one of the tables crafted by

Rommel's imprisoned Panzers, reading my way into the future. That chair and table, the hagiography of the windows made simple in annunciations of flushed light, the dove descending, Mary in blue, Isabel and her abandon, a treadle sewing machine, all are a permanent inscription in my formation as a reader. One could speak of palimpsests on which our journeys as readers continue to be recorded, layer upon layer. When gathered together in bound signatures and tested for heft, where will they fall open?

A Relative of Chekhov, a Cousin of Chaliapin

There was a funeral in progress when we arrived to visit Chekhov's grave, and the uniformed guard at the gate shook his head, *nyet*, we could not come in. *Nyet.* A Soviet official was being buried. The host of mourners in the distance was relatively small, and the cemetery, situated next to the gold-domed Novodevichy Convent, seemed large enough to accommodate a dozen such funerals—or certainly this one funeral and the two of us, my interpreter Lidiya (not her real name) and myself. But the chauffeurs, glaring in our direction, had pulled their ZILs and Chaikas into a tight line near the entrance, and the guard beside the fluttering black bows on the temporary metal gate shook his head again and repeated, *Nyet.*

It was a word that I had heard repeatedly in what was then the Soviet Union, and it was delivered that particular September morning with a tonal flatness that barely acknowledged our presence.

After a pause, there was the briefest of explanations in answer to Lidiya's quizzical look. Her small stature and aura of innocence had perhaps loosened the guard a bit. I asked her to explain to him that I was a visitor to their country—as if that weren't obvious in my clothing and speech—and did not know when I would be able to return to Moscow. Could he please make an exception and let us visit Chekhov's grave for a few moments? As Lidiya conveyed this to him, he quickly resumed his official posture, shaking his head again and looking away into the autumn morning. The bottom line was still *nyet*; power was burying one of its own and it required the whole cemetery, glasnost or no. This was in 1987, two years after Gorbachev initiated his proposals for transparency, openness, glasnost. These proposals were in addition to the series of political and economic reforms, perestroika, that he undertook.

Lidiya looked at me as if to say that she was sorry but could not push my request any further. My schedule, governed for the most part by the itinerary of my delegation, had delayed me in offering this small gesture of homage to Chekhov. Now it was time for me to leave Moscow for a trip to Leningrad (since restored to its original name, St. Petersburg) with the delegation. I had gotten a cab for the ride to the cemetery, splurging a bit to give us an extra half-hour or so with Chekhov's wan ghost. Lidiya had come along as a favor to me, something extra beyond her duties as interpreter. She had been assigned to my delegation, which was associated with one of the programs at the 1987 Moscow International Book Fair.

The cab fare now seemed a foolish extravagance, especially in the face of the exorbitant fee I had recently been charged for four phone calls back to the States—less than an hour's worth of time, but I had neglected to consider that my connection was through the switchboard of my hotel, the Rossiya. Lidiya had attempted to help me appeal the charge, but again the word was *nyet*. Guard at the gate, hotel agent behind glass window, various functionaries everywhere, it didn't matter, *nyet* was usually the word.

Though I did not know Lidiya well, I sensed that she wanted somehow to apologize for her country, or at least for a system so anxious about power that it would deny both citizen and visitor this brief gesture of homage. It seemed to me a natural thing to do—pay my respects to the good doctor and ponder for a few minutes those perfectly attenuated, bittersweet moments he had offered in his plays and short stories.

My inclination was stronger perhaps because I had just seen *Dark Eyes*, with Marcello Mastroianni, before leaving the States. Mastroianni had caught with a wonderful whimsy and soulfulness the character of the philanderer Gurov (Romano in the movie version), who was so smitten with the married Anna Sergeyevna in this adaptation of Chekhov's story "The Lady with the Pet Dog." The film put me in mind again of the writer whose work had suggested to me long ago an affinity with the complex humanity of the people I now found myself among. So why not go out to the cemetery next to Novodevichy Convent and nod my regards?

Part of what Chekhov suggested to me involves an aspect of the Russian character that seems chronically vulnerable to systems of power. Almost any power—whether that of higher government, minor bureaucrat, hotel doorman, or check-out clerk in a hard-currency *beriozka* shop—seemed to be regarded as something that must be obtrusively displayed, as though any less force would result in its loss.

Even in its milder incarnations that impulse took the shape of a maddening rigidity. I had noted on my visa application that if my schedule allowed I would like to visit Yasnaya Polyana, Tolstoy's ancestral estate some 200 kilometers south of Moscow. When I applied to the Moscow office of Intourist, the state tourist agency, for help in arranging transportation and permission to visit Yasnaya Polyana, I was told *nyet*, the house was closed for renovation. I would not have to go into the house, I said, it would be pleasure enough simply to walk around the grounds. To suggest that this was not just a whim, I handed the agent, who was fluent in English, a *National Geographic* article I had brought from the States. It included photographs of the birch-lined road leading to the house, along with a map that I thought would be useful if she did not understand where it was that I wanted to go. And there was a photo of the Count himself.

Nyet.

Later that week at a reception at Spaso House, the US Embassy, given by then–US ambassador Jack Matlock for the members of my delegation and the Russian officials involved in the Moscow International Book Fair, I mentioned my disappointment regarding Yasnaya Polyana to Matlock, who had studied Russian language and literature at Duke University. He seemed immediately to understand the appeal and inherent goodwill of such a visit and was concerned that my request had been denied. He asked an aide if they would contact the Soviet minister of culture and see what could be done. I was to call the aide the next day for further instructions, which I did and was told to go back to Intourist and explain that if there had not yet been a message from the Ministry of Culture, the agent was to call the ministry to discuss the matter.

At Intourist I found myself face to face with the same agent I had dealt with before. She listened impassively to my story and then told me again that the house was being renovated. I repeated that though a tour of the house would be a welcome enhancement, my request was simply for a solitary walk through the woods and fields of Yasnaya Polyana. Please call the ministry if there had not yet been a message. She said she would do so and notify me. The slow burn that she radiated when I took out my notepad and asked her name—partly as a bluff but partly to have a reference if I had to inquire again—told me that I had crossed the line between nuisance and territorial threat.

If she left a message for me at my hotel, I never received it, but I was by then too frustrated with the tangle of communication to pursue it. I could have called the embassy again, but it seemed an insignificant matter in the context of their larger concerns. Among other things, there was a new embassy building going up, and electronic bugs had been discovered in the construction.

As for the guard at the Novodevichy cemetery, maybe it was a simple matter of strict orders from higher up. But by that time I

A Relative of Chekhov, a Cousin of Chaliapin

had been in the Soviet Union long enough and had been turned away or patronized by so many similar individuals that I took it as yet another instance of a stone-cold functionary so obsessed with what little power he had, and at the same time so beaten down by the system that maintained the hierarchy of that power, that he could not form a decent response.

The quality of spirit that I found in Lidiya and other friends I made during my short stay lies at the center of the paradox that observers of Russian culture have often found so perplexing and yet poignant. It is a commonplace to note the great bear of a heart that the best of Russians possess, a rugged thing with enormous hunger and capacity. One apprehends it, at its best, as a depth of feeling and understanding. A readiness to celebrate the spiritual. A ground of sadness underlying a sweetness of demeanor, such as Lidiya's. (Along with numerous others, she had lost her parents in the long siege of Leningrad by the Nazis.) The kind of wistfulness that runs through Chekhov. But alongside this hunger and capacity in the Russian soul is lodged also a trait of conformity and submissiveness that has historically invited abuse. As the poet Andrei Voznesensky told Robert Cullen, writing in the *New Yorker*, "It's the instinct of a thousand years of peasant culture. One God, one leader—the czar."

An equally succinct and disquieting expression of that habit of mind was evidenced in news reports that the director of a technical school in Lyubertsy, near Moscow, threatened her staff with disciplinary action if they did not bring in absentee ballots marked for Vladimir Putin in the March 2012 election. "We need to submit to one commander in chief, like in the army," she said. "Someone commands, and like soldiers we follow." More recently one of Putin's deputy chiefs of staff said, "No Putin, no Russia." And in Russia's July 2020 plebiscite, intended to keep Putin in power until at least 2036, the editor in chief of *Yegoryevsk Today*, a small state television station southeast of Moscow, ordered her staff not only to vote but to make sure they voted in the town of Yegoryevsk, owing to a need to mobilize enough voters in the district.

When I returned to Moscow after visiting Leningrad I had a few extra hours before I had to begin preparing for departure from the Soviet Union. On a lark I suggested to Lidiya that we go and give it another try at Novodevichy. I still wanted to pay my respects to Chekhov.

It was a Tuesday, not a day one would expect large crowds or official funerals. Our spirits were buoyant. There were still clusters of yellow and reddish orange leaves on the trees, and the sky was a template robin's egg blue. The gold domes of the old convent shone with what seemed an added luster in the autumn light.

As we approached the gate I was brought up short by the fact that a guard was there. We had seen people walking to the cemetery and entering with what I took to be complete freedom, but I had not seen the guard. Lidiya told me to wait. The guard came and spoke to Lidiya. Her look of gaiety faded. It was the same guard who had turned us away before. Lidiya told me that he said we needed a blue card. Tuesdays were set aside for relatives of the dead, and we had to have a blue card. He had not said it yet, but the effect was the same. *Nyet.*

Lidiya looked completely puzzled, perhaps panicked. Maybe she sensed that I was going to challenge the guard. Aware of her sensitivity and fear, I held my first impulse in check and asked her if she would explain to the guard that this was my last day in Russia and I had hoped to pay homage to the great Russian writer Chekhov.

She spoke again to the guard, who had betrayed no emotion, no indication that he remembered us from before, even though I wore a black eye-patch, which probably would have registered in his memory. He shook his head. *Nyet.* We had to have a blue card, be a relative of the dead.

I asked Lidiya to point out that there were only the two of us and the cemetery did not seem crowded. We would stay inside only a brief time and then leave. I had to catch a plane that evening. *Nyet.*

As Chekhov said of his character Belikov in "The Man in a Shell," "the only things that were clear to him were Government regulations and newspaper notices in which something was forbidden. When some ruling prohibited high school students from appearing on the streets after nine o'clock at night, or some article censured carnal love, this he found clear and definite: it was forbidden, and that was that" (translation by Avrahm Yarmolinsky).

Beyond the gate I saw another guard. The uniform he wore seemed to me a cut above the one on the guard of the great void of nothingness. I am not sure exactly what came over me, but I broke past the guard at the gate and caught his superior, or so I perceived him, by the sleeve. Whether or not he understood my English I do not know, but he looked at me with total incredulity as his comrade grabbed me by the arm and hauled me back to the gate.

It was all Lidiya could do to keep her composure. She put her hand on my arm and looked at me as if to say please calm down or you will be detained and miss your plane. But I could not leave without one last try. Why could I not settle for the positive things I had experienced—the Russian friends I had made, the picnic at Peredelkino in the woods near Pasternak's former dacha, the looks of gratitude when I gave a group of scholars a sheet of postage stamps bearing Faulkner's image. Or the time one of our hostesses went into her kitchen and returned to slip the little package of sage into my coat pocket when I asked her what seasonings were in the pork roast at our farewell dinner, the toasts that went on into the evening, or simply the autumn light that was filtering through the birches and lindens? I must have felt compelled to try to make some small gain against the recurrent *nyet*.

And in doing this I was apparently willing to risk seeming melodramatic, incontinent, one needing to be handcuffed. Please tell him, I asked Lidiya, that I understand it is a day for relatives. But tell him also that my adult life has been given to the cause of literature and in that sense I *am* a relative of Chekhov.

Lidiya must have seen that I was going to get into trouble if she did not speak for me. She turned to the guard and spoke her few sentences softly. Beyond her through the gate I could see a few people here and there along the paths. As she finished this final plea for the newly appointed relative of Chekhov, I could see the least hint of amusement forming on the guard's face. But his smile was of a smugness that would have approached contempt had he not been so taken with his own cleverness. He looked into the distance just over our shoulders as he replied. Lidiya translated for me as we walked away.

"Yes," he had said, "and I am a cousin of Chaliapin."

Chaliapin, the famous Russian opera singer. Chaliapin who sang with Caruso at La Scala, a Pavarotti, an operatic Elvis of his day.

One of the posters I brought home depicts a rubber stamp whose handle and base are shaped like a squat, featureless man. His suit and matching tie are the purple of a generic rubber stamp. The Cyrillic letters to be imprinted by the stamp serve as the poster's caption, running diagonally across the man's head: БЮРОКРАТ. BUREAUCRAT.

Underneath the descending stamp is a green leaf—symbolic, one assumes, of the life and hope of a society. The thinness of the shadow between stamp and leaf tells us that the deadening mark of the bureaucrat is imminent. (Were one to create a similar poster today, the image of the bureaucrat would be replaced by that of the kleptocrat: клептоцрат.)

The poster is dated 1987, the year when the words "glasnost" and "perestroika" were beginning to attain currency in international news. Those words have little or no meaning today. Nor was there much chance, we see now, that they would result in any lasting value, given the lack of assertive pursuit.

Commenting on why Russia keeps drawing him back, why he keeps returning, John le Carré's character Barley in *The Russia House* (set during the time of my visit and including a scene at the book fair) says, "Because of their making do. . . . Because they can rough it better than we can. . . . Because God always found excuses not to come here. . . . Because of their universal ignorance, and the brilliance that bursts through it. . . . Because they try so hard to be like us and start from so far back." Then his plaintive conclusion, "Because of the huge heart beating inside the huge shambles."

Observers are divided over the question of whether there is any hope for meaningful change within those shambles. Putin's self-nominations and rigged elections in 2012 and 2020, the enveloping culture of corruption, the pervasive government control of the media, the jailing—and in some instances the murder—of government opponents, the dependency of the courts on the Kremlin, all would seem to suffocate any hope. But the protests over Putin's rigged elections, the Pussy Riot events, the outrage over the unsolved murders of Kremlin opponents Anna Politkovskaya in 2006 and Boris Nemtsov in 2015, the 2006 polonium poisoning in London of Alexander Litvinenko and the 2021 imprisonment of Alexei Navalny—are evidence, especially in Moscow and St. Petersburg, of traction for forces of change. As David Remnick said in his 1993 book *Lenin's Tomb*, "Perhaps one day Russia might even become somehow ordinary, a country of problems rather than catastrophes, a place that develops rather than explodes." One hopes. But clearly, though, Putin's behavior is increasingly czarist, revanchist, and intransigent. Especially after his invasion of Ukraine.

Among my mementos from Soviet Russia is a small ceramic bear. I call him Boris, though he is not Boris Yeltsin's namesake, nor Pasternak's. I found him on a square of green felt that the artist had spread on a curb in Moscow's Izmailovsky Park. Boris was a member of a large menagerie, but he had a quietly commanding presence that set him apart. I bought him in a heartbeat.

Boris is sitting on a stool which you cannot see because of his big legs, his spiffy double-breasted split-tail coat, and his cello, to which he is applying the bow at a casual angle. His coat is of a handsome bold plaid in cerulean blue. The strings and f-holes of the cello are of the same color. The *f*s are not quite in balance, but Boris is making up for that with a look of composure he manages in a way that does not conceal his pleasure in the music he makes.

All told, he is about three inches high, but it would be amiss to take the measure of his music by that scale. Probably he is both a relative of Chekhov and a cousin of Chaliapin, for the somber-sweet music that I imagine him playing on his violoncello opens a clear pathway for Chekhov's quickened spirit, and it is a safe guess that Chaliapin is picking up the melody somewhere in the near distance. It is folly to think that the spirit of that music, in whatever way that spirit might be expressed, could ever hold sway in the halls of power and governance—or inform in any definitive way the agendas there. But it is certain that to neglect what it celebrates is to settle for an impoverished sense of life and diminished hope.

Heroes

Once when I was staying at the Rossiya, the massive hotel in Moscow adjacent to Red Square, the lobbies and hallways began filling with throngs of older men. I called them the heroes, because they wore medals and decorations. Some of them had medals not only on their lapels but also across the fronts of their jackets. For the most part their jackets were civilian—either so stiff they seemed to have been cut from tin that morning or so misshapen and threadbare as to impart an almost clownish poignancy to the decorations—but the number of military uniforms also among them made it obvious to me that they were all veterans, and by their age I could tell that they had fought against the Nazis in the Great Patriotic War, which is how they describe the Second World War. They had come from all over what was then the Soviet Union to see who was still on the list of the living.

The manner in which they had faced the prospect of oblivion some forty years earlier was of course in no way clownish or lacking in resiliency. They had had no idea that Hitler was going to turn on them and invade their country. But they put their unprepared army and their fierce winter against 3 million Germans and turned them back, though at an enormous cost. The 900-day siege of Leningrad alone was enough to count as a war in itself. At the end of it all—Leningrad, Paris, Berlin—we dropped confetti in our streets; the Russians brought the flags of the German Wehrmacht to Red Square and burned them in front of Lenin's tomb.

And now the heroes were back in town with a party or two in mind. Several times I came upon sections of the hotel where the handles of the hallway doors were looped with chain and locked. The image was a bit unsettling, but I realized that this was just their way of establishing a private conference area. Like many mechanical things in Russia, the normal door locks didn't work. At other times the elevators in certain areas were closed to public use. No notices, no explanations. I could sometimes hear the sound of singing and music coming through the shafts or from distant reaches of the hotel (which is now razed but then had 1,000 rooms and was the largest in Europe) and I would try to imagine a room full of men with medals and bright ribbons on their coats celebrating the wonder of survival.

After dinner one night when I returned to the Rossiya, there was music and singing in the main ballroom. The heroes were having another party. As I looked through the heavy smoke of the room, I could see only perhaps a half-dozen women among the throngs of men. Some of the women were dancing, but for the most part the heroes were dancing with each other. They were in twos and threes or in circles dancing dances I had seen only in movies with Omar Sharif or Yul Brynner. Though the band was not prepossessingly colorful or demonstrative, the music was from the rugged lyric heart of Mother Russia.

Occasionally one of the heroes would rush over to someone he had apparently just recognized in another group and they would embrace in great bear hugs, sometimes with one picking the other up into the air like a wrestler but without throwing the uplifted one to the floor. There were vodka bottles everywhere and count-less toasts, but I did not have the sense that the party was an orgy of drink and food. It was not as though there weren't any drunks, but by and large the heroes were moving about wonderfully well.

Among them I spotted two men whom I was sure I recognized; I had taken a photograph of them the day before. In fact, I can call up the details of that earlier meeting very vividly even now. The two men bear the look of what I would guess to be Kazakhs, a mix of Turk and Mongol. So they have come from Kazakhstan to Mos-cow with their fur hats and their gray chin beards and their med-als to be with their comrades. My guess also is that they have just come out of St. Basil's Cathedral, for I have stopped them on the street between the Rossiya and St. Basil's and they have in their eyes a combination of reverence and slight amusement at the fanciful domes, which might seem like a child's watercolor creation were it not for a final artistry of design. It is to this famous symbol that I gesture, by way of engaging their attention and, I hope, their trust. I have in mind taking their photograph, of course, but a camera is not to be brandished about carelessly in this country. They smile and nod their heads also toward the colorful domes and towers.

Holding up my camera, I point to their medals and then ges-ture toward St. Basil's to let them know I would like it as a back-ground. They understand, smiling again and nodding agreement. To affirm for them their relative standing in all of this, I point a second time to their medals with respect. They have about a dozen of these apiece—three on the right lapel of each of their coats and the remainder on the left breasts. Most of the medals are attached to decorative ribbons. When I back away and raise the camera, they draw themselves up just slightly, nothing approaching a rigid military stance, and their faces adjust accordingly, the smiles giving way to what would be a near neutrality of regard if it weren't for the hint of an absolute, and shared, confidence in their footing in the world. It is not a look or posture that in any way threatens my sphere of being, but there is no mistaking the response that would come if I inclined that way toward theirs.

As I study the photo now, I notice there is a loose affinity in the way they have arranged the medals on their right lapels. Perhaps the arrangement and its placement on the right follows a protocol, because the same three medals appear there on each of them. But the particular arrangement varies on each—that is, if there is a protocol, one of these Kazakhs has gotten it mixed up. What I choose to imagine instead is that the three medals bear special significance to them personally, and in dressing out for this reunion of the heroes they followed each other's example only loosely, there being no impulse toward strict conformity in their buoyant fierce hearts.

Perhaps because he is grandfatherly and his look—more on the Turkish rather than the Mongolian side of the Kazakh mixture—places him closer to me in the cultural geography, I sense more of a potential bond with the man on the right. I think too that the sash he has wrapped around his midriff has a folkish kind of élan that appeals to me. It is dark blue with thin red and gray stripes running on the bias. His pants are tucked into his boot tops, as are his friend's, and he sports a handsome walking cane. Cradled partially underneath his roughly knit woolen outer garment is a package bound with twine—meat of some kind, I would guess. Sausage probably, for there are grease spots coming through the paper wrapping. At the moment I am feeling shame for having offered him and his friend some kopecks for allowing me to photograph them. They are shaking their heads no, and I am fumbling for something else to offer them that would be acceptable as a gift. As it turns out, I have a couple of lapel pins that I just bought— Lenin's profile set in the enamel of a bright red-ribboned bow. The Kazakhs are delighted, and as I leave them they are huddled together comparing their pins, proud and happy patriots. Heroes.

From my place just inside the large entrance door of the ballroom, I could see these two men dancing, and for a moment it was as though I had discovered old friends unexpectedly, though I did not attempt to greet them or make my presence known. Apparently the dance involved a couple's alternating between engagement with the immediate group and then a temporary separation from the group for an informal, though obviously not improvised, series of movements in concert with each other. It may have been, though, that this pattern was simply a variation that my two Kazakhs had worked out spontaneously.

To say their dancing was something like that between Anthony Quinn's Zorba and Alan Bates's character is to identify something of its quality, but also to miss something essential. There was nothing staged or self-conscious here, nor was there anything manic about it. Smiles and laughter occasionally, but no cinematic Greek passion. For one thing, these two men were both older than Zorba. More to the point, they were dancing, I imagined, to something in their shared past that was given a keener context in this gathering of old comrades, but also something they could honor and celebrate outside the toasts and vodka talk, outside language. Or at least that was what I sensed in the occasional solemnity that I detected in the moments when they looked to each other for cues to the dance's next progression. I am not suggesting an informing backdrop of heroism or valor; it might well have been that they simply survived a war together and went home with an increasing sense of life's sweetness.

Whatever the case, I was a rapt witness to the occasion of their return to that interior, and I had the distinct feeling that, both in spite of and as part of the general pandemonium of the room, there were in their movements at times the vague tracings of ceremony.

That feeling gave me all the more reason not to make my presence known or in any way interfere in this reunion, but before leaving the ballroom I did maneuver myself a bit closer to the group they were dancing with, close enough to notice that the grandfatherly one was wearing his sash with the red and gray stripes. And he had his walking cane, which he sometimes held over his head during the dancing as a kind of balancing device. I could not tell if they were wearing their Lenin pins.

It seemed to me the next day that the heroes were thinning out, going their separate ways to Kazakhstan and Armenia and Moldova. But it was not a mass exodus, for there was still the occasional flash of medals on a coat in the elevator or in the gloomy hallways. Whatever the case, the ballrooms cleared to the degree that my group and I felt comfortable enough to have our own party, which is to say request a table in the main ballroom and join in the general party of the evening. But I had seen the heroes and knew that even at its most intense pitch ours could be only a half-note of the thing that the heroes had sung and danced to in that same room.

Still and all, we had a passable rock and roll party. The band had discovered something between Elvis and the Eagles, and they nearly wore it out trying to find the ultimate imitation on both ends. I danced with every woman at our table and then with a Russian woman in a fake leopard-skin skirt. While we were on the floor, another couple closed in on us so as to form a tight circle. The man had on ill-fitting polyester pants and vinyl boots that we left behind twenty years ago in America. But he could jump into the air like a Cossack and kick the cheap boots out in front of himself without missing a beat. I could not tell if he was challenging me or making a bid for the attention of the woman in the fake leopard skin. I tried the Cossack leap and kick several times, and I think that maybe I came close enough to gain his approval. At any rate, he smiled as the band finished out the song.

When the band started up again, the Cossack motioned me to his group. I did not have a partner, but that did not seem to matter. We were dancing in a circle, and I was supposed to follow the Cossack kick for kick. In the midst of all of this I looked to the large entrance door where I had stood the previous night watching the heroes. A man was standing there, peering into the ballroom. He had on the clothes of the provinces, some far country, and then I realized he was a hero.

I wanted him to be the old Kazakh with the sash around his waist. There was a similarity of build. The clothing too bore a likeness, except this man had no sash or cane. And the beard was a different style. Still there was a vague familiarity about him. He had to be one of the heroes from the party. Maybe one of the ones who had lifted a comrade into the air and whirled him around. But his manner now was tentative as he moved into the room a few steps. Why had he not worn his medals? Where were the other heroes?

The beat had shifted, intensified, and the Cossack looked to me to match his leaps and kicks. I had found a rhythm of movement that would work with the music and his challenge, and I had gotten bold enough to initiate moves of my own. The circle alternated between our examples, though his continued to be smoother, more dramatic. Someone touched my arm. The woman in leopard wanted to enter the dance again. All the while I could see the hero looking around the room for the celebration he had been a part of the night before. My impulse was to get his attention and motion him into our circle, but his gaze was somewhere else. Something in the music or our dancing was driving him into himself by its strangeness.

He surveyed the room one final time and turned toward the door to leave. There was now a trace of forlornness in his face. I could see it also in his posture as he walked slowly away. The band went into an all-out attempt at Jerry Lee Lewis—"Great Balls of Fire"—and the circle took me to where I had only a glancing view of him. Again I felt an impulse to call to him to join our dance.

But what were we with our unfamiliar music, our stories that could never fill him with renewed wonder? Which of us could lift him into the air, shake and turn him like a hero? I went back to my dancing. The Cossack was in a frenzy, his vinyl boots nearly a blur. The leopard woman was smiling, trying to be friendly to the Cossack's earlier date, a small, wiry woman also in polyester, but it was clear that the dance cards had been revised for the evening and there was going to be a discussion.

The large door opened again. In the brief moment before anyone entered, I realized that I was watching in anticipation, wanting it to be the hero returning with a brigade of his comrades and my two friends from Kazakhstan to claim a table or the entire ballroom, but it was a group of Muscovites looking for a rock and roll party. The heroes had all gone home, or were in their rooms packing their things—sausages, Lenin pins, little dolls called *matryoshkas*, carved of wood and nested one within the other like Chinese boxes. A stray hero might be wandering the hallways, looking for a party, a music he could understand, but he was still secure with the rest of them in the list of the living.

The band had turned to the Eagles, and the singer was having a go at "Hotel California." *Some dance to remember*, the song dreamily went, *some dance to forget*. The Cossack must have figured it was a stretch but probably his only chance at a slow dance that night. He was in a deep embrace with the leopard woman, trying to make the best of the jerky rhythm.

Damn You, Love

AUTHOR'S NOTE: This essay was written on assignment for *Esquire*. The editors entitled it "The Wicked Witch of North Carolina," but I have retained its original title here. It is revised to indicate the date of occurrence.

14–401.5. Practice of phrenology, palmistry, fortune-telling or clairvoyance prohibited. It shall be unlawful for any person to practice the arts of phrenology, palmistry, clairvoyance, fortune-telling and other crafts of a similar kind in the counties named herein . . .

This section shall not prohibit the amateur practice of phrenology, palmistry, fortune-telling or clairvoyance in connection with school or church socials, provided such socials are held in school or church buildings.

That was the law, or at least it was the law in 65 of North Carolina's 100 counties, when these events occurred in 1976.

If you were in one of those counties then, you'd better watch out in whose presence you rub skulls or throw tarot cards or sort through the entrails of chickens for answers to life's mysteries—unless, of course, you're at a school or church social and provided such social is being held in a school or church building. "If the law supposes that, the law is a ass, a idiot," you may say along with Dickens's Mr. Bumble. Nonetheless, it's all there in the book—tucked securely in the Cumulative Supplement of *The General Statutes of North Carolina* between a statute that prohibits the tattooing of "the arm, limb, or any part of the body of any other person under eighteen years of age" and a statute prohibiting the distribution of certain deleterious food such as ground glass at Halloween and all other times. In between is Section 14–401.5, no phrenology, palmistry, clairvoyance, fortune-telling or raising people from the dead, except as noted.

It seems unlikely that a former go-go dancer and Sunday school teacher should run afoul of the law on this count, but that is what happened to Joann Denton in 1976. I first heard about it on NBC News. After clearing away the heavy stuff—Carter, Jackson, and Udall, each predicting success in Pennsylvania, and the prospect of coffee jumping to two dollars a pound—John Chancellor added this note of human interest: a North Carolina woman, Joann Denton of Morganton, had been charged under an unusual witchcraft law with having accurately predicted the date of another Morganton woman's death. Mrs. Dorothy Ramsey had died on April 10, the date predicted by Joann Denton at a séance, and a complaint charging Mrs. Denton under the witchcraft law had been signed by the deceased woman's daughter, Kathrin Carpenter.

At that the needle on my receiver twitched a notch or two—not so much at the fact of human loss as at the mention of North Carolina, which is where I live, and at the bizarre character of both the law and the circumstances of the death. Alcohol and drugs were mentioned. Not long afterward, *Newsweek* carried a report and a photo of witch Denton sitting in a wicker rocker, holding a plastic skull. The magazine suggested that Joann Denton and Fred

Ramsey, the dead woman's husband, had gotten together before his wife's death to lay carpet in some apartments owned by Joann Denton (one of which she rented to Fred Ramsey) and that they had gotten very chummy. I wanted to hear more.

As it turned out, it was not the prospect of learning about cultural patterns through all this trashy behavior, as Larry McMurtry's Sam the Lion would call it, that led me to drive 170 miles west to Morganton and seek out the witch. My real purpose in seeking out the witch had to do with Scott Fitzgerald.

Why Scott Fitzgerald? What could he share with Joann Denton, Fred and Dorothy Ramsey, and the other dramatis personae that fate cast for this little contemporary ritual drama? Scott Fitzgerald wrote mostly of the glamorous, and these Morganton people, as will soon be evident if it has not already been guessed, are decidedly *un*glamorous. One of them, in fact, continues to encourage the public to regard her as a witch, and most of the others seem damned to various levels of alcoholism, catastrophe, error, or a general lack of normal behavior. So why call on Scott Fitzgerald?

Well, that is a curiosity on my part that I will reveal more about later. It has to do with rooms. For the present let me say merely that the places involved are close together: Morganton, North Carolina—where Joann Denton the former go-go dancer and Sunday school teacher and present witch lives—and Asheville, North Carolina—where Scott Fitzgerald took Zelda for psychiatric care at Highland Hospital while he waited in a room at the Grove Park Inn and tried to write and recover from what he called "emotional bankruptcy." Close together, but separated by a mountain and the Eastern Continental Divide, which means if you pee on the Morganton side of the Divide, it, the pee, flows to the Atlantic Ocean, and if you pee on the Asheville side it flows to the Mississippi River. Two different waters, two different worlds. And besides that, Scott Fitzgerald had style. He wouldn't jazz around with a witch, especially not one who has gotten all this attention for having struck upon the precise day of another woman's death. Of which more later.

Dorothy Ramsey, thirty-eight, whose death the witch had accurately predicted, had been separated from her husband, Fred Ramsey, forty-two, for some six months, was not physically present at that séance back around March 20 during which her death was predicted. In fact, her *spirit* was not even supposed to have been there. It was Buddy Carpenter's spirit they were trying to stir up. (Carpenter had committed suicide the previous fall by shooting himself in the head after he and his wife, Kathrin, broke up. Kathrin Carpenter, you remember, is the daughter of Dorothy and Fred Ramsey. She was the one who signed the witchcraft complaint that led to Joann Denton's arrest.)

According to Fred Ramsey, the request to communicate with Buddy Carpenter was from someone else, but the session itself was his idea and was held in a vacant apartment next to his apartment, which he rented from Joann Denton the witch. Ramsey says that he and his brother, Melvin, had been drinking earlier in the evening and for amusement he suggested that they go to the vacant apartment for a séance. Joann Denton had come by for a visit and so happened to have her séance table in the car. There were several others present, but I'll leave them out right now since the scene is already burdened enough. Melvin got into the room a little late and, upon learning that they were trying to talk to the dead Buddy Carpenter, put his bottle down and said, it is reported, "Yeah, I see ole Buddy sitting over there in the corner right now." "Not yet, Melvin. Turn the lights out," quoth witch Denton. A drunken sense of humor is to be responded to in essentially the same manner all the time, whether you encounter it while dancing in a go-go joint or raising the dead in a vacant apartment.

I don't know how a car wreck got into that particular séance, but the suggestion of a car wreck somehow came up and Joann instructed the participants to think *car wreck*. Fred Ramsey reports the following exchange:

FRED RAMSEY: "I see a black car going over a cliff."

JOANN DENTON: "What else?"

F. R.: "A puff of smoke."

J. D.: "Do you see a number?"

F. R.: "Zero one five."

J. D.: "Anything else?"

F. R.: "Nothing."

The 015 was Dot Ramsey's house number backward. Since the separation from Fred, she had lived at 510 Mull Street. "I probably made it up," Ramsey told me, and then, using a logic that escaped me, he added, "I loved my wife so much I had her on my mind." That, by his testimony to me, was as close as he got to his wife during this or any other séance. Earlier reports indicate that he said he saw his wife in a vision during the séance—one account has him describing her running off the road with two men in a black car and disappearing in smoke—but he now maintains that he did not see an apparition of his wife during the séance and does not believe that she knew of any death prediction.

Not so, says witch Denton. Her story is that after the vibrations started coming she "made communication with Buddy's [Carpenter's] spirit and Fred said, 'I see him!'" Whatever the Carpenter vision promised seems to be lost or forgotten (like Coleridge's interrupted vision of Xanadu, perhaps, and his wild singer: "Close your eyes with holy dread, / For he on honey-dew hath fed, / And drunk the milk of Paradise"), for almost simultaneously another presence intruded. "I feel a coldness," said the witch to the watchers. "It is death. Look over my shoulder and see who it is." Picking up on this fresh transmission, Ramsey began describing a woman with dark hair and then, according to Joann Denton, sobbed, "It's her."

"Who?" they all asked.

"Dot."

After this identification by Fred Ramsey, Joann Denton says she divined the future and named the day of Dorothy Ramsey's death, April 10, saying it would probably be in an automobile accident—settling on that device maybe because a burning-black-car-with-two-men apparition was described during the sitting. I don't know. No one tells the same story twice. There are also conflicting reports as to whether Mrs. Ramsey actually learned of the prediction and, if so, from whom, but it appears evident that she did hear of it, either from Ramsey himself or from her sister Marie, who was also present at the séance—or most probably from them both. Whatever the source, giving Dorothy Ramsey the news was evidently something like feeding a live Jimi Hendrix concert into an old drive-in-movie speaker.

Big Bird and Cookie Monster were in town on April 10, the foretokened day, and Mrs. Ramsey had promised her daughter, Kathrin Carpenter, and Kathrin's little girl that she would go along with them to see the show. Kathrin's grandfather drove them to pick up Mrs. Ramsey, but when they arrived at her house on Mull Street she said she had changed her mind. "She was nervous," Kathrin recalls, "and she just kept taking pills and taking pills to calm her nerves down." Mrs. Ramsey had in fact been involved in an automobile accident that week but was uninjured. "Fred and his girlfriend are trying to get rid of me," she told them. "What girl?" the grandfather asked.

"The witch," she replied. (There were rumors, you will recall, that the Denton-Ramsey relationship went beyond the normal landlady-tenant agreement, but both deny it.) Mrs. Ramsey wouldn't get in the car, so the others went on to see Big Bird and Cookie Monster without her.

That evening the grandfather came out and told Kathrin and her boyfriend, Mark Allen Basham, that he had just heard that an ambulance was on its way to 510 Mull Street. He heard it on his police scanner. He asked them wasn't that Dot's address. By the time Kathrin and her boyfriend got to Mull Street, the ambulance was gone. There were suicide notes and various pills around. A little over halfway to the hospital the medics put code blue on their transmitter, indicating that Dorothy Ramsey's vital signs were failing and that Joann Denton was about to get her certification as a witch.

The pink carnation with the card inscribed "From a Friend" the next day was perhaps what stirred the dead woman's relatives into action and ultimately brought the matter before the magistrates. The funeral parlor had instructions to pin the flower to Mrs. Ramsey's lapel. When Kathrin inquired of the florist who the friend was, she was told Joann Denton. "It was just like it was some kind of a hex," says Kathrin. The flower was snatched from the casket and the witch hunt was on. Or maybe there was an entire corsage. It would take that many to supply the various narratives I heard. One was that Marie, Dot's sister, found Joann and threw the pink carnation at her, telling her, "If you're going to witch somebody, witch me!" Another one was that Mark Allen Basham, Kathrin's boyfriend, found Joann and threw the pink carnation in her face. That one is probably closer to the truth, for Joann Denton did take out a warrant against Basham for allegedly threatening her life. More recently she included him in some predictions she made public on a WTOP talk show in Washington, DC, auguring that he will die in a car wreck within a year. But the best one was that James, Dot's brother, tracked the witch down—her car, a Gremlin, is easily spotted: it carries a license plate reading ANN-38 (her bust line, she says) and the inscription "Gray Shadows" on the side—and upon finding her in a parking lot set the pink carnation afire and threw it on her. I like that one, mainly because I like to imagine what a pink carnation looks like burning. It was the one Fred Ramsey told.

Kathrin went before two magistrates before getting one to issue a warrant against Joann Denton. The charge was not murder but violation of the previously discussed North Carolina General Statute 14–401.5, which carries only a misdemeanor penalty. The law was enacted in 1951 for the purpose, according to some of its sponsors, of regulating bands of roving gypsies or other "traveling rogues and fly-by-night con artists who separated the ignorant and superstitious from their money," and it obviously doesn't worry itself with the niceties of the First Amendment. That problem notwithstanding, the law was remembered by an eager detective in the Morganton Police Department and hauled out when Kathrin came in following the discovery of the pink carnation and requested action. The ignition of the pink carnation had not been enough. The first magistrate refused to issue a warrant, being unsatisfied that there was probable cause to believe that a crime had been committed. According to Kathrin, he told her that the only way to get rid of a witch was to "drive a silver stake in her heart." She told him that was a vampire, but he still wouldn't issue the warrant. The second magistrate she went to was apparently satisfied of probable cause, and a warrant was issued against Joann Denton on April 14.

The charges were dropped by the state on April 26—the DA opining that Mrs. Denton was not *practicing* one of the enumerated arts within the meaning of the statute (she did not charge a fee) and that the charges were based on "pure hearsay, and without benefit of sworn statements from any persons who were actually present during the alleged prediction." But not before the wire services and other media, ever alert to any small flash of promise out there on the horizon, be it *ignis fatuus* or bona fide fire, had picked up on the happenings and started beseeching Joann Denton for her story. "Double, double, toil and trouble," she told them. "Fire burn and caldron bubble." Or something like that. She planned to keep on exercising her "special God-given talents of fortune-telling and clairvoyance in Burke County, North Carolina." Earlier, Laurie Cabot, self-styled witch of Salem, Massachusetts (who later boiled a brew that ended a vexing ten-game losing streak for the Boston Red Sox), had offered to send financial assistance or even bring part of her coven down to help out. On the other side, a preacher from South Carolina was offering to aid the police in further investigation, after which he wanted to burn the lady, quite literally.

After the state's dismissal of the charges, Joann Denton went on television and among other things predicted that on August 11, 1976, her mother, Mrs. Clarence Denton, seventy-three, would die. (You should by now detect a pattern emerging. Joann is, as they say, into death. Especially car wrecks and cardiacs. Also blood and blood disease. Her milder auguries let you off with only adultery, divorce, and such. About the best you can hope for in her divinations is the prospect of going on a trip in the near future—but be careful on the road.) "It hurt me," her mother says. "I don't like that publicity." But she is apparently not taking the prediction seriously. "I don't plan to go until the Lord calls me," she insists.

It was around the time of this matricide fantasy that I was preparing for my road trip to Morganton to sit in on a séance or two and then take the witch over the Divide to Asheville to see if we couldn't get a fix on Scott Fitzgerald.

Here's the way I got ready to go off and see the witch:

- I went to some lectures on psi (the science of parapsychology) that the Smithsonian was sponsoring in Chapel Hill.

- As it turns out, I live seven miles from the psi center of the cosmos—Durham, North Carolina. The Institute for Parapsychology, which grew out of J. B. Rhine's early experiments at Duke University, is there (now the Rhine Research Center and no longer associated with Duke). Also in Durham was the Psychical Research Foundation.

- I went there to talk with director William G. Roll (M. Litt., Oxon.) and research associate Blue Harary. Though their main concern was "whether man survives the death of his body," they were interested in any aspect of psi and were very generous with their time and reading material, among which was an article by Roll, "Suggestions for Exploratory Investigations of 'Mediums,'" that afforded the kind of practical information I needed—for example, "at the time of the session the medium should not know the name or anything else about the inquirer"—and told me generally how to behave.

– I wrote the letter Joann Denton told me she would need in order to read my full fortune. I wrote it on the unlined paper she had specified on the phone, but I decided to deliver it by hand so there would be no postmark. I signed it "A Seeker."

– I bought some masking tape.

– And then with an élan that inspires me to this day, I bought a pair of 100 percent cotton beltless pleated slacks by Ralph Lauren for Polo that cost me three times what I ordinarily pay for cotton slacks. They reminded me of Gatsby.

To reduce the chance of a staged séance, I went to see Joann Denton a day early. At the same time of my registration at the Morganton Holiday Inn, two other Seekers—I was to later learn—checked in, none of us knowing the others. One was a man fifty or so, dressed in a tweed jacket, who ordered a beer in the motel restaurant and was told the same thing I was told when I had ordered a beer—that he couldn't have one, it was against the law. He could legally bring in a bottle of hundred-proof liquor in a brown paper bag and drink it until he was cross-eyed, but he couldn't have a beer. Fred Ramsey must have written the bill.

The first session was at Joann Denton's house, which is called Gray Shadows, same as her car. Though it was dark—about ten o'clock at night—and I had already covered my Chapel Hill windshield sticker and license plate with the masking tape, I parked down the street and walked to the house. The medium, remember, should not know the name or anything else about the inquirer. Joann Denton let me in and introduced me to Mike. He was the man in the tweed jacket who couldn't get a beer at the Holiday Inn. That scared me. I am what the psi people call a "paranoid." I

Damn You, Love

am very sensitive to confluent events, synchronicity, coincidence. Already that day I had stopped for gas at what turned out to be the station where Joann Denton buys her gas. An attendant there told me the witch had seen a car wreck in his palm and a fatal blood disease in his girlfriend's palm. A few months later he had totaled his car and then a few months after that the girlfriend got weak, went to the doctor, and learned she had leukemia. I could have stopped at any of a number of other stations.

Joann Denton lives alone, unless you count her chihuahua, Little Shrimp, and Joelene, her "other spirit from a previous life." Some visitors claim to have seen Joelene, but she does not communicate audibly with others, though she will tilt tables, as she did when I was there, and speak through Joann Denton. Joann says that she has known since the age of six that she has psychic powers. Her mother told me that Joann was a normal child and all this witch stuff is foolishness, especially the prediction of her, the mother's, death. Joann Denton's childhood was spent in Burke County about five miles from Salem, where she went to school. As an adult she is five feet three inches tall, has black hair, and appears to have posted her bust measurement on her license plate about right, though one should not infer that she still automatically qualifies as go-go dancer. Time's winged chariot is hurrying near. Still, there are a lot of less attractive witches out there shaking it for the horny and humpbacked.

As it turned out, I didn't get my full fortune told. After talking with the gas-station attendant, I didn't much *want* my full fortune told, but that was not the deciding factor. Mike, the victim of the beer laws, had more pressing needs. He was having trouble with his family and the family business. Ronald Hearn, well-known London psychic, had given him some help, but air fare between Philadelphia, Mike's home, and London was getting too expensive. At about the time Joann Denton got in the news, Mike had a trip to Florida that would allow him to dogleg by Morganton.

One of Joann's followers, Audrey, was also at the seance that night. We went back to the séance room to see what Mike ought to do. He told Joann that he wanted to ask for guidance from his mother and father. They are both dead. Joann told him to write their names on separate pieces of paper and place the one he wanted to talk to first face down on the table. And to tell her which one it was. It was his mother. We removed all our jewelry and watches, and Joann took the pendulum off the clock and turned out the lights. After ten or fifteen minutes of vibrations and unanswered questions it became evident that Mike's mother didn't want to tell him what to do. He put his father's name on the table and we waited awhile longer. Joann said she felt the father's spirit in the room and for Mike to speak to him. "Touch my nose, Pop, if you are present," Mike told him. Nothing. Audrey said she felt a chill on her left arm. Joann told Mike to go ahead and ask his father the questions. The questions took a half hour or so. What Mike wanted to know was whether the family would ever work in harmony again—his brothers had voted to kick him out of the business—and if he should try to sit down with them and talk in peace or if he should go to the company attorney. Still nothing. Audrey said she felt a chill on her left arm. Joann said that Joelene had come into the room and would answer the questions by tilting the table—"three times for a yes, two for a doubtful, and one for a no." Mike asked the questions again. Try to sit down with his brothers and talk in peace? A firm single tilt. Go to the company attorney? Three quick tilts. So much for brotherly love in Philadelphia.

Given the general lack of drama and verve during our first session, I didn't think Joann Denton would travel over the mountain to Asheville. Maybe what swayed her was the ceiling falling on Fred Ramsey. It happened in the apartment he was renting from her. It happened in fact on the night Mike was having trouble talking to his parents. I think it restored her faith in herself, especially her retributive powers. She and Ramsey had not had kind things to say about each other since his wife's death. She later intimated that the ceiling falling on his head was a kind of spin-off from the thwarted energy of her attempts to get Mike's folks to come across. It put Ramsey in Grace Hospital for two days—and I think brought her

Damn You, Love

and her retinue to Scott Fitzgerald's room in the Grove Park Inn. What I had in mind from the start was, in my estimation, the ultimate test of any medium's powers. Say Joann was, in an initial session in familiar surroundings, able to strike fairly close to my age and give me a fortune-cookie kind of reading, as she had. Fair enough. But to negotiate the Continental Divide, come into a strange room and demonstrate that she could deal with the fire of the world beyond would require the purest kind of visionary filament. What I wanted, of course, was some illumination from Scott. I would know if it was truly his.

The reason I would know is that I have spent time in out-of-the-way rooms such as that one, rooms where people whose work I care about came and left something. It's my theory that gifted people generate a tremendous energy—though it need not always be manifest on the surface—and a residuum of that energy is left behind in places, especially rooms, where the gifted burned up part of their gift.

And there was no doubt in my mind about that being his room. I had a book with a photograph of the Grove Park Inn with his X's marked on the windows. Plus Mrs. Neilson, a fine lady who had worked at the inn since before Scott was there, *told* me that was his room. She knows, she used to read discarded manuscript pages of his stories from the wastebasket when she'd get it out in the hall. The same furniture was in the room, too, she said, except the rocking chairs have now been taken away. Probably they didn't do much to rest Scott's soul. He felt as if he had cracked up. The orgastic (Fitzgerald's word) future didn't look so good anymore. His first summer at the Grove Park, 1935, blew away in a beer fog. He sat around and made lists, lists of "cavalry leaders and football players and cities . . . and lists of women" he'd liked. In order to sleep he took Luminal and Amytal. Or a young married woman from Memphis he'd taken up with. Zelda was in a private hospital in Baltimore, claiming she was "in direct contact with Christ, William the Conqueror, Mary Stuart, Apollo," and so on. He brought her to Highland Hospital in Asheville the next year, 1936, but things never got to be the way they were. "I'm going to fix everything just the way it was before," Gatsby had said in another context. "She'll see." But Daisy never saw.

I told Joann Denton and the five acolytes whom she had brought—four women and a man—only that the person was dead and had expended considerable psychic energy in the room and I felt some of it was still around. I said that I would help with some more information if they got hot. For a psychometric object I had chosen *The Crack-Up* and had a copy of it in a brown bag to place on the table. Most mediums prefer some personal object that has been touched a lot by the person whose spirit is being sought, and I explained that though this object had not been touched by the person, I was satisfied he had a strong emotional investment in it and that it had something to do with what had gone on in the room. I also had a book—I had taped the spine—containing photographs of Fitzgerald.

Of the five psychic trainees, it was Daniel who impressed me the most. He looks like Elvis Presley and works in a piano factory for a living. I hope he is the one who gets to run the sander over that exquisite curve in the grands. I am convinced he has psychic powers. He was the first one to do the automatic writing that night.

Joann got vibrations almost immediately after the lights were turned off, and Daniel started thrumming like the Grateful Dead's big McIntosh amps warming up before the Dead come on.

"He's in here. It's like a heart—throb, throb—feel it in the table," Joann said.

Audrey said she felt a chill in her left arm.

"Spirit of the man, send us a message. Take the pen and take his hand and send us a message."

I should tell you that there are a lot of moans and deep guttural utterances from the dedicated when things get to going in such a session. The sounds are like those you hear from people who throw themselves to the ground at fundamentalist revival meetings or, in their milder versions, like the sounds of a woman nearing orgasm. Or at least that, the latter, is how Virginia and Carol sitting next to me sounded.

By that time Daniel was scribbling away. "He's sending you a message, Danny. Write it down," Joann would say. "Uhn-uhn," Daniel would answer. "Write it down, Danny." "Huhn," Finally he slammed down the pen: "No. No!" "The message wasn't good," Joann said, "but he was a very distinguished-looking man. He was well-thought-of. A neat dresser."

"Tore me all to pieces," said Daniel. "I'm soaking wet. Feel the sweat off my head, you think I'm kidding. Joann, run your hand down my back. Feel how wet I am."

"What does it say?" Audrey asked, and then answered herself: "He says DAMN to start with."

"And there's a L-O-V," said someone else.

"Yeah, wait . . . DAMN YOU, there's Y-O-U."

"Look, it says, 'Damn You, Danny'!" joked Audrey.

"Naw, don't say that," Daniel told her seriously.

"It's something about *love*," one of the other women offered.

"'Damn You, Love' is what it says," Joann informed us. "I told you it was two women. It's pertaining to a love affair. You don't always get a full word in automatic writing."

"Damn You, Love," Audrey said, rubbing her left arm.

"By God, that's right," agreed Daniel. "Tore me all to pieces."

What follows you'll have to take my word on. Before I told them at the end of the evening that it had been Scott Fitzgerald I was seeking, Daniel asked me if the name "Tony" meant anything to me—that was a name that had come to his mind during the writing, he said. I told him I didn't think so. He asked me what about "Gloria"—that name had come to his mind, too. The effect of those two names coming together in my own mind so unsettled me that I couldn't take much notice of the brief second sitting we had. Somehow Daniel had come up with the two main characters of Fitzgerald's *The Beautiful and Damned*, Anthony and Gloria Patch. Anthony is actually called Tony at least once in the novel—by a man in a bar—toward the end, when alcoholism has ruined him. The name Gloria has also been used to refer to the unidentified young married woman from Memphis with whom Fitzgerald had a disastrous affair.

Let me say again that I don't think that these people—Joann Denton, Daniel and his wife, Virginia, Carol, who was the sitter during the second session, Audrey of the frissons, and the woman who drove the station wagon—knew where they were coming. I don't think they knew that Scott Fitzgerald ever stayed in Asheville, North Carolina, or that they would have taken note even if someone had told them. They did not see the book in the paper bag or the photographs. Maybe my psi "paranoia" is such that I'm not qualified to make any final assessment. But it seems that somehow they were able to enlist from the spiritual residues of that room a wrath and frustration and an oxymoronic kind of attitude that were characteristic of Fitzgerald. And characteristic of a lot of us, of course, so that doesn't elevate ANN-38 and her followers into the spiritual elite.

When my clairvoyants were leaving to go back over the Divide and through the mists that hang in the low places of the mountains of western Carolina at night, I heard one of them in the parking lot below asking one of the others—I promise you—to tell her again who Scott Fitzgerald was. He was the one, I wanted to tell them, who once wrote that "the test of a first-rate intelligence is the ability to hold two opposed ideas in the mind at the same time, and still retain the ability to function. One should, for example, be able to see that things are hopeless and yet be determined to make them otherwise." "Damn You, Love" comes in the back door of that idea, yet is fully at home within it. But all that would have been rather abstract for people who are accustomed to dealing with the world in terms of flaming pink carnations, falling ceilings, car wrecks, chills, and so on.

Still and all, I could hope that Joann Denton would come to think in a different way of those split souls who come to her and want to talk about getting things together again. Maybe she would have pondered it and resolved to be easier on them and their families. But by the time I thought of that, Joann and her cortege were crossing the Divide, where the topic of conversation has to do with the flow of things depending on which side you are on. They would probably agree, though, that we all are boats against the current, borne back ceaselessly, though we beat on.

One Corner of Yoknapatawpha

During the autumn of 1929 when Faulkner was writing *As I Lay Dying* to the hum of the dynamo in the powerhouse where he was working the night shift, my father, some twenty miles away in Panola County, Mississippi, had another kind of dynamo in his head. He had retrofitted a 1927 Model T Ford with axle spacers and what were called "motor car" wheels that enabled it to run on a railroad. My father described his new creation as slow and noisy, the latter owing to poor alignment of railroad track and wheels. The tires had burned off his "T-Model" when the family home in Batesville caught on fire the year before, and he decided to convert it into a vehicle that he could take into the hunting grounds of the Tallahatchie River bottom land, or as it was sometimes called, the Big Bottom.

This was the bottom land along the Tallahatchie River in Panola County, which is at the eastern edge of the Mississippi Delta and adjacent to Lafayette County, where Faulkner lived. By the time of my father's youth in the late 1920s much of the timber in the Big

Bottom had been cut away by lumbermen, my grandfather among them, but there were still some big woods remaining that were rich with game. The spur-line railroad (known as the Dummy Line by locals), on which timber had been transported from the Tallahatchie Bottom to the Darnell Lumber Company sawmill just outside Batesville, was soon to be abandoned, and my father could motor down to a hunting camp that he had established. At the end of the rail line there was a wye that would get him and his hunting pals turned around and headed back to town.

Though it is not likely that Faulkner was present to hear the new sound of my father's "T-Model" in the woods that year—he was working steadily on *As I Lay Dying* during the hunting season— Faulkner was in fact a regular in those very woods. Beginning as early as 1915 or so and continuing through the mid-1930s, Faulkner had come to hunt, and drink, with the hunting parties that General James Stone, father of Faulkner's friend Phil Stone, held annually at a camp five miles from my father's camp in the Big Bottom. Faulkner would later draw on these experiences at General Stone's camp in his creation of "The Bear" and other sections of *Go Down, Moses* (1942), as well as in *Big Woods* (1955). Each year Faulkner's fictional hunters "would drive away to Jefferson, to join Major de Spain and General Compson and Boon Hogganbeck and Walter Ewell and go on into the big bottom of the Tallahatchie where the deer and bear were. . . ." Major de Spain had a hunting camp in the Tallahatchie River bottomland, limning the hunting camp of his real-life counterpart General James Stone.

The Tallahatchie River serves as the northern border of Faulkner's fictional Yoknapatawpha County. On the map of Yoknapatawpha that he drew for *Absalom, Absalom!* (1936), Faulkner identifies the location of Major de Spain's Tallahatchie River camp in the northwest quadrant of the county. On a later map, annotated for Malcolm Cowley's *Portable Faulkner* (1946), Faulkner altered the "Fishing camp" designation of his earlier map to read "Hunting & fishing camp where Wash Jones killed Sutpen [*Absalom, Absalom!*]. Later owned by Major De Spain."

Faulkner's annotations on both maps identify this particular corner of Yoknapatawpha as the setting not only of *Absalom, Absalom!* but also "The Bear," as well as the short stories "Wash," "A Justice," and "Red Leaves." All of these works, with the exception of "Wash," hark back in one way or another to the time when Chickasaw and Choctaw Indians were still present in the region, both before and after the land cessions of 1830 and 1832 wherein they ceded their land to the federal government. Issues of land ownership, conflated later with issues of slavery, are fundamental concerns in the two short stories, though those issues are not expressed in the heightened moral register that Faulkner summons in *Absalom, Absalom!* and "The Bear." In the latter, the protagonist Ike McCaslin is so conflicted that he questions the right of even the Chickasaw chief Ikkemotubbe to have sold land to his grandfather. This vexation is deepened further by Ike's discovery in the plantation ledger that his grandfather fathered a daughter with one of his slaves and later fathered a child with that same daughter. Neither of whom would he formally acknowledge as his child. Ike comes to regard the land as forever tainted by the injustice of slavery. He is profoundly aggrieved too by the destruction of the wilderness that has been home to the bear Old Ben and the primitive spirit that the bear represents.

Faulkner named his "apocryphal county," as he called it, after an actual river, the Yoknapatawpha, which was the Chickasaw name for the river that is now called the Yocona, a corruption of Yoknapatawpha. A further variation appears on an 1861 map I located at the US Corps of Engineers in Vicksburg, Mississippi. The river is identified as "Yoch na pata fa." Above it, and sited on the Tallahatchie River, is the now vanished town of Panola. (My father's camp, General Stone's camp, and the confluence of the Yocona River with the Tallahatchie River were all within a radius of less than ten miles.)

Faulkner's fictional county, according to notes Malcolm Cowley recorded after a conversation with Faulkner in 1948, "borrows scenes and features from three real Mississippi counties." If

Faulkner cited those three counties, Cowley did not record them, but I am confident that one of them is Panola, if on no other basis than Faulkner's many visits to the Stone hunting camp and the identifiable "scenes and features" that may be observed.

Looking back on that time and place, John Cullen, a farmer and one of Faulkner's fellow hunters, says, "There never was and never again will be on this earth such a paradise for hunting dogs and men as the miles and miles of great virgin forests and jungles of the Big Bottoms [*sic*]." Cullen, who collaborated with scholar Floyd Watkins on a book of reminiscences, *Old Times in the Faulkner Country*, recalls further that "a man could travel for miles under the open timber and never see a road. Ole Colonel [*sic*] Stone owned a good bit of land, the place where he built his camp. . . ." In his book *My Brother Bill*, John Faulkner also recalls the Stone camp, "By the time Bill was grown and began deer hunting, our timber [in Lafayette County] had mostly been cut. That's why he had to go to the 'Big Bottom' for his story. . . . The Delta begins thirty miles to the west of us. . . . It was here, just beyond Batesville at General Stone's cabin, that Bill first went on his deer and bear hunts and wild-turkey shoots."

Faulkner's visits to Stone's camp and the bottom lands of the Tallahatchie, it seems to me, exposed him to a milieu that, while not radically unlike the one in and around his Oxford, nonetheless extended and enhanced his sense of Yoknapatawpha's potential as a fictional ground. First there was his exposure, as a hunter going in and out of the woods on a log-train, to the dynamic created by the mechanical force of the lumber industry meeting the resistance of nature. Faulkner was especially sensitive to this tension. That nature was near-primordial—dense virgin timber, swamp, canebrake, briar thickets, diverse wildlife—and it was on the verge of extinction: "that doomed wilderness whose edges were being constantly and punily gnawed at by men with plows and axes."

When I say that Faulkner was exposed to a somewhat different milieu here, remember that Panola County and the Tallahatchie Bottom are where the Delta merges with the hills, a landscape unlike that of the predominantly hill country in Faulkner's La-fayette County—and one bearing a slightly different cultural stamp. A liminal zone, if you will. A space betwixt and between, a state of transition and ambiguity. Panola County embraces both the Delta and the hills. In one direction the horizon seems limitless, in the other the hills begin closing in. To say that the one encourages expansiveness and the other clannishness is perhaps too reductive, but it begins to suggest possible tendencies.

Remember too that Faulkner's Oxford was, and remains, a university town and as such offered a degree of refinement that Panola County lacked. That is not to suggest that Faulkner's experience in Lafayette County was limited to town life. Again, these various differences were not profound in their every expression, but there were significant nuances and shadings, and Faulkner was keen on gradation—and ever alert to possible strategies for extending the dramatic reach of his Yoknapatawpha.

After my father told me of his motor car and the proximity of his hunting camp to General Stone's camp, it occurred to me that I should try to find the site of the Stone camp and inquire among the locals concerning their memories of the place. Clearly Faulk-ner had found in the surrounding Big Bottom—in its larger history of slavery and in the immediate drama of its diminishment by ax and plow—one of his most resonant and compelling emblems of struggle and loss. Nowhere in Faulkner's fiction do we find a more plaintive rendering of what he called "the human heart in conflict with itself." In "The Bear," there is Ike McCaslin's plea, "Don't you see? This whole land, the whole South, is cursed, and all of us who derive from it . . . lie under its curse? . . . Don't you see?" Ike repudiates his heritage and retreats into a life of near penury in which "even if he couldn't cure the wrong and eradicate the shame . . . at least he could repudiate the wrong and shame, at least in princi-ple." In *Absalom, Absalom!*, Sutpen, with his band of Haitian slaves, wrests from the wilderness a plantation, Sutpen's Hundred, and then goes on in his attempt to subjugate all around him as though the world were a slave quarters. And there is Quentin Compson's conflicted cry in *Absalom, Absalom!* when asked by his roommate at Harvard why he hates the South: "I dont. I dont! I dont hate it! I dont hate it!"

I wanted to locate the old Stone camp also because I was curious to learn more about my own family's investment in that part of my home county. My grandfather had cut and milled timber in the Tallahatchie and Yocona Bottoms (and hence was a villain, by implication, in Faulkner's indictment regarding the diminishment of the wilderness) and he later owned farmland there. With directions my father had provided and with the help of Panola County's chancery clerk Brooks Vance and some of the elders around Panola, I found the old campsite one spring in the late 1970s. As it turned out, the hunting lodge itself, or clubhouse as the hunters called it, was still standing. It was in the middle of a big soybean field. In any direction you turned there were silos, John Deere tractors, and more fields under cultivation. Except for a big oak tree that had been left standing beside the house, the only thing that would suggest there was ever a woodland there was a line of trees that formed a horizon along the Tallahatchie River less than a mile away. The effect of the whole scene on my sensibilities was not unlike what I would have felt had I discovered one of the whaleships on which Melville's *Pequod* was modeled, the *Acushnet*, say, or the *Essex*, stranded somewhere in the whaling grounds.

I was aware too of another phenomenon having to do with literature and place. If I had never read Faulkner and you took me to this bean field and told me all about it and the clubhouse, which resembled the house of a tenant farmer more than a hunting lodge, I would nod and agree, but in truth it would be little more than just another bean field to me. When an author sets a narrative in motion around an actual place that we recognize, however, that place becomes invested with a kind of extra-reality, if the fiction has established a valid claim on our imagination. In addition to its own history, the place takes on that of the fiction as well. All this is by way of telling you something of the effect the sight of the old clubhouse and its surroundings had on me. For other readers that sensation might come in Pamplona, Yasnaya Polyana, the moors of Yorkshire, Birnam Hill (Birnam Wood, alas, like Tallahatchie's Big Woods, has also vanished—and not merely to Dunsinane gone), or wherever literary pilgrimages might lead. I cannot claim that my vision was of the intensity of Ike McCaslin's when he returned to the hunting camp for the final time in "The Bear," but perhaps I had a whiff of it: "The wilderness soared, musing, inattentive, myriad, eternal, green; older than any mill-shed, longer than any spur-line."

One of the old-time Panola County natives I talked with, Jim Hancock, remembered the days when he sometimes went for as long as two months without seeing anyone else in the Big Bottom. He was a trapper, and his trapping season usually began around the middle of November, after his father's crops were laid by, and extended until early February. During that time he worked alone out of a ten-by-twelve-foot tent, trapping mink, beaver, racoons, and occasionally otter. Hancock told me he once trapped a white otter, which the game warden said was "a freak of nature, just like Babe Ruth." Born in 1904, Hancock was trapping regularly by 1923, and until his retirement fifty years later he was engaged in something related to the Tallahatchie Bottom, either trapping or logging or clearing land and farming it.

Though he knew who Babe Ruth was, Jim Hancock had never heard of William Faulkner. He did, however, remember the day that General Stone died in the clubhouse of the Stone hunting camp, which was near where he trapped and hunted and later worked in logging camps, one of my grandfather's included. He said somebody came and told him that old General Stone had died in the clubhouse—that they had been drinking and gambling all night and he had died that morning and that the camp cook wouldn't go back in the house as long as the General was in there dead.

At one time General Stone owned some 2,000 acres in Panola County, most of it in the Tallahatchie Bottom. His father had begun acquiring land when he settled there in the mid-1850s. There were also considerable land holdings on Stone's mother's side of the family. Her great uncle Potts is reputed to have owned 100 square miles of land along the Tallahatchie River. Potts's sons, Theophilus and Amodeus Potts, known as Buck and Buddy, owned the land on which General Stone's hunting camp later stood. (A Potts family member was a partner with my grandfather in ownership of a parcel of that same land in later years.) They served Faulkner as models for his characters Uncle Buck and Uncle Buddy, the former of whom was Ike McCaslin's father, and it was his entries in the plantation ledger that led Ike to his realization concerning his grandfather's treatment of his slaves.

General Stone was born James Bates Stone, his middle name most likely in honor of Reverend J. W. Bates, for whom the town of Batesville was named. His birthdate is listed as 1856 in *Biographical and Historical Memoirs of Mississippi* (Chicago, 1891), but his tombstone in Batesville's Magnolia Cemetery is marked 1854. (It is a stone's throw, so to speak, from my family's burial plot.) After graduating from Kentucky Military Institute, Stone entered law school at the University of Mississippi, though he withdrew after a few months. Dan Ferguson, former mayor of Batesville, who knew both the Stone and Faulkner families, told me that Stone "read the law" in order to qualify for the bar, a not uncommon method of self-education.

In my youth I visited Ferguson's farm with his son Danny for horseback riding and camping trips. In later years I learned that the farm had been a part of the Stone landholdings in Panola County and that the dilapidated log house where Danny and I sometimes found shelter from the rain was Stone's birthplace.

Danny once found a pewter flask in a hidden crevice of the house. I'd venture a guess that someone was maintaining a private stash for drinking on the sly. A fondness for strong drink ran in the Stone family. And, as I've mentioned, drinking was one of the main draws at Stone's camp, along with the gambling and hunting. Jim Hancock noted that he heard that Stone had been drinking heavily during the night before his death. The *Panolian* of November 26, 1936, carried the announcement that "while on a hunting trip at his lodge west of town Monday morning about 10:30, seated in a chair, Gen. James Stone, age 83 years, passed peacefully to the Great Beyond." This would have been the Thanksgiving hunt. A month later, at the Christmas hunt, one of his sons, James Stone Jr., died also. According to the *Panolian*, the cause of death was a heart attack, but one of my grandfather's former associates, Selwyn Shuford, told me that the younger Stone had been drinking all night and was found face down in the pool of water surrounding an artesian spring outside the lodge.

As for further potential effects of alcohol, one of my father's most vivid memories of his hunting days in the Bottom was of the time that hunters from the Stone camp came to his camp late one night with a corpse:

> While we were camped at the Fuller Field one winter, an ice storm covered the earth. Some people from Sardis [a town in Panola County near Batesville] were camped in the old Stone clubhouse. One night about 12 o'clock midnight some of them came to our Fuller Field camp with a corpse loaded on a mule-drawn wagon. They had been drinking corn likker, the man had put his lips to a poison bottle of it, and died. They wanted us to haul the corpse to Batesville and send it on to Sardis. The rails over the bridge were coated solid with ice, and the only way for us to cross it was for one of us to go ahead of the "T Model" and clear the ice from the rails.

The man undoubtedly suffered poisoning, immediate or accumulative, from moonshine that had been distilled through an automobile radiator, a not uncommon distilling process, but one that resulted in toxic whiskey, owing to the lead residue in the radiators. The automobile radiators were cheaper than copper stills, and irresponsible or ignorant moonshiners sometimes resorted to the cheaper method.

Whether General Stone and Faulkner were present at the Stone camp on that particular hunt, I do not know (nor am I suggesting that Faulkner drew on that experience in creating the Bundren family's travails in conveying Addie Bundren's corpse by mule wagon to be buried near her family in *As I Lay Dying*; mule wagons were more common than FedEx is today). But the drinking at the Stone camp was legendary, and Faulkner of course had a lifelong battle with alcohol. Dan Ferguson jokingly told me that he saved Bill Faulkner's life. He said that General Stone once brought Faulkner into Batesville from the camp and asked him to get Faulkner a cure for the hiccoughs. Faulkner mentions the hiccoughs incident in a letter (undated) to his agent's assistant:

"I am now working at a story which the POST should like. I am sorry I didn't see you again [in New York]. I got into my usual drinking gang [at the Stone camp] and drank pretty hard for a time after reaching home [from trip to New York], was taken sick, quit drinking, had hiccoughs for forty-eight hours, and as a result I am expecting to be notified that I have permanently ruined my stomach and must live from now on upon bread and milk."

Ferguson said that General Stone told him he would have brought Faulkner into town sooner but Faulkner "had been down there drunk for two weeks." Ferguson went to Will Cox's drugstore, but Cox was out of town, so Ferguson had to call a druggist in nearby Como to come to Cox's drugstore and fix a "secret" remedy. Faulkner lived to tell the story, though he recast it considerably. In "A Bear Hunt," published in the *Saturday Evening Post* in 1934, the character Lucius Provine is cured of his hiccoughs in an encounter with Chickasaws who have been led to believe that Lucius is a revenue agent investigating their moonshine whiskey–making operation.

Stone established his first law practice in Batesville in 1880, and he was engaged in farming and business interests as well. His newspaper notice in an 1891 *Panolian* states that his law practice embraces the "Circuit and Chancery Courts of Panola and adjacent counties and in the Supreme and Federal Courts of the State." Stone often rode alone on horseback to get to these various courts of law, the locations of which were distant enough that he sometimes had to make camp overnight. It is said that he claimed

John Wilkes Booth once stumbled into his camp. True or not, the narrative impulse and sense of adventure evidenced there were undoubtedly aspects of General Stone's character that enthralled the young William Faulkner and contributed to his creation of Major de Spain.

Soon after Stone's notice appeared in the *Panolian*, he moved with his family to Oxford. Among other considerations, there was the fact that the Federal District Court met there. Stone had served as general counsel to the railroad in Batesville and would later serve in the same position in Oxford, hence the title "General," according to some accounts. He retained ownership of his lands in Panola until financial difficulties forced him to begin selling land in order to pay drainage taxes. But he continued to maintain his hunting camp there.

In addition to Stone's hunting camp, the Dummy Line railroad and other features of the logging operations provided Faulkner with images for the vanishing wilderness of *Go Down, Moses* in which "the diminutive locomotive and its shrill peanut parcher whistle" could occasionally be heard by the hunters as it carried the cut timber out of the Big Bottom. (Before the Dummy Line was abandoned by the logging company, and before my father had his motor car, the distant whistle of the logging train served as a geographical marker for my father and his fellow hunters, in addition to their compasses.) Major de Spain had arranged with the lumber company for the hunters to ride the train to a stop near the camp in the same way that General Stone had an agreement that allowed him and his hunters, including Faulkner, to catch rides to and from an official stop near the clubhouse. I found an entry in the Panola County chancery records in which General Stone deeded sixteen-hundredths of an acre to Batesville Southwestern Railroad Company in 1911. This would have been the land required for what was designated as Stone Stop, which consisted of a small building used for storage beside the railroad. According to my father, one of the train conductors was Jim Stone Moseley, named in honor of General James Stone.

The log-line junction, Hoke's, which figures prominently in "The Bear" was undoubtedly modeled on the junction and sawmill that Darnell Lumber Company operated in Panola County just west of Batesville about eleven miles from the Stone camp. Faulkner and his fellow hunters came from Oxford to Batesville and then loaded their camp supplies on the log train at Darnell's for the journey to Stone Stop. From there they would go by mule wagon to the clubhouse.

The old Chickasaw-Choctaw Boundary, which divided the lands of those two nations, still serves on Panola County land maps and chancery records as the northeast boundary line of the tract of land on which the old clubhouse was situated. The Chickasaws, according to federal treaty makers, described the boundary line as follows: "Beginning at the mouth of the Oak-tibby-haw and running up said stream to a point, being a marked tree, on the old Natches [Natchez] road, one mile southwardly from Wall's old place; thence with the Choctaw boundary and along it westwardly through the Tunica old fields, to a point on the Mississippi river about twenty-eight miles by water, below where the St. Francis river enters said stream on the west side."

The white surveyors who came along after those land cessions of the early 1880s employed a similar method of description; that is, one based on existing landmarks and without any apparent concern that those landmarks might shift or disappear over time. Their determination of the beginning of the boundary in a document of field notes from the General Land Office, dated October 16, 1836, reads as follows (with misspellings preserved): "Boundry Line Between: The Chickasaw and Choctaw Cessions in Mississippi biginning at a point on the East bank of the Mississippi River directly opposite the house where a Mr. Philips once lived which is siuated in the town of Helena in the state of Arkansaw. Set large post and erected mound as per instructions." They then trekked through briars, cane, and swamp for their survey.

If you begin at the point across from where a Mr. Philips house was situated, and on the Mississippi side of the river where the mound was erected, and make your way along the old Choctaw-Chickasaw Boundary for about twenty-seven miles, you'll come to the site of the Stone hunting camp: Section 32, Range 2 E, Township 28. The structure, as of this writing, has fallen into a state of desuetude, and in fact is probably flooded, the tragedy of which I will address later.

I would like to be able to tell you the name of the person who held the original patent on that tract of land, but I am unable to do so. Most likely it was a Choctaw, for the tract lies on the Choctaw side of the boundary. I can tell you the names of a number of Chickasaws—Shana, Untishetubbe, and so on—who marked their X's and received a pittance for sections of land on the other side of the boundary in this immediate area. Many of those sections were later owned by General Stone (and some subsequently by my grandfather), in addition to his ownership of the clubhouse tract. The Panola County *Chain of Titles* goes back only to 1862, and the Department of the Interior was unable to help me find the patent. It would not have surprised me, though, if they had told me that the original patent on the clubhouse tract was held by Ikkemotubbe. He was the Chickasaw chief, you'll recall, in Faulkner's fictional account, from whom Sutpen got his 100 square miles, Sutpen's Hundred, "for money or rum or whatever it was."

And so Faulkner's chancery would read Ikkemotubbe, Sutpen, de Spain, and finally the name of the fictional Memphis lumber company to whom Major de Spain sold the timber rights in "The Bear." Actual lumber companies began arriving in the Big Bottom around the time Faulkner indicated in "The Bear," the late 1880s. Before they arrived, however—and at approximately the same time the fictional Sutpen came storming in, the early 1800s—a more sympathetic figure passed through and was so taken with the unspoiled quality of the place that he later wrote an account of one of his experiences there. The traveler was John James Audubon, and in one of his essays he gives directions for finding "the Swamp" so that students of nature could visit and observe its "rare and interesting productions: birds, quadrupeds and reptiles, as well as molluscous animals, many of which . . . have never been described."

Audubon's essay concerns a panther hunt. In the course of one of his rambles, he chanced upon a squatter's cabin on the Cold-water River (the Coldwater joins the Tallahatchie less than ten miles west of where the Stone clubhouse and my father's hunting camp were located). Audubon was so engaged by the handsome pelts on the wall and the squatter's descriptions of the area's wild-life that he asked the squatter to be his host and guide for a few days. The next morning while they were feeding the hogs, the squatter told Audubon of a large panther that had been ravaging his live-stock: "In addition, the Painter, as he sometimes called it, had on several occasions robbed him of a dead deer; and to these exploits the squatter added several remarkable feats of audacity which it had performed, to give me an idea of the formidable character of the beast." Audubon was fascinated and offered to assist him in hunting down the animal. After gathering enough neighbors and dogs for a hunt, they charged off into the swamp. There follows an enthusiastic report of the hunt and the wilds through which they traveled, the upshot of which was the death of the panther. After-ward the hunters made camp, killed a small deer for their meal, and sat around telling tales, singing, and passing the flask.

The problem with regard to attacks on livestock was a common one in the region. Not only were there panthers, but bears posed a problem as well. And in addition to preying on livestock, they would ravage stands of corn. One such example is contained in a letter (*The Civil War Letters of Edward Randolph Neilson*, unpublished manuscript edited by John G. Nelson III) posted by Edward Neilson from his plantation Bearsden, which was within ten or fifteen miles from the hunting camps of Stone and my father: "Tallahatchie, 30th of July 1861. . . . I think we will make corn enough to do us if the bear do not eat it up. In the last three or four days several have commenced upon it and they are destroying it very rapidly."

Posted the next day:

> This evening about sundown just as I was going to supper
> I heard Griffin shoot down in the corn field and call for the
> dogs. I got my bear knife and went to him in a hurry. He
> was setting old Jimmy [the name of his gun] for a bear and
> while he was at it, one started to come over the fence close
> by him. He shot him on the fence and he rolled over inside
> but got up and got outside. We put the dogs after him and
> he went about 150 yards in the cane and stopped for a fight.
> I gave Griffin the knife and I took the gun. It was dark when
> we got to him. He ran one of the dogs right up to me and I
> shot him [the bear]. The dogs all seized him and Griffin gave
> him the knife. He caught Venus after he had been knifed
> twenty times and got her down when I gave him a blow on
> the head with the barrel of old Jimmy which knocked him
> down and made him let her go. I never saw a bear stand as
> much knifing. It took at least fifty blows and they well aimed
> to make him lay still. I do not know how bad Venus is hurt.
> It was so dark I could not tell. The bear was very large and in
> good eating order. He was destroying our corn very rapidly.

Before reading this account, I had at times wondered if Faulkner's
rendering of Old Ben and the bear's capacity to survive for so long
what the hunters mounted against him was perhaps a tad hyper-
bolic. One of Old Ben's paws is mutilated from a trap in the distant
past, he has been assaulted by countless hounds, and at the time of
his death it is found that he has collected fifty-two slugs under his
hide over the years. (Readers will recall that Moby Dick carried the
remains of broken harpoons from previous encounters with whal-
ers. And it is reported that the whale Mocha Dick, the probable
model for Moby Dick, had numerous rusty harpoon tips beneath
his skin.)

Neilson's hunt involves a relatively short time and distance. His
bear went only 150 yards from the fence before he stopped to fight

Venus and the other dogs. In contrast, the climactic hunt for Old Ben is of long duration and distance. Granted, those conditions are in the service of dramatic effect, but Faulkner's drama is in fact consistent with the reality of many bear hunts. Among the papers from my uncle Damon Page's archives is a letter that a man who farmed in the Tallahatchie Bottom wrote to one of my uncle's in-laws, a Mr. Prince. Besides being faded and difficult to read, the letter is further compromised by misspellings and inconsistent punctuation, but it will serve to confirm further Faulkner's accurate sense of the duration and rigor of typical bear hunts. It is posted from "South Panola Co Mississippi, September the 30th 1867":

I will tell you of our hunting excursions we lost our start dog last spring and could not dance a lick until the last weak Mr Clinton and myself cut out last weak up to ascues bluff [probably near Askew, which coincidentally is my father's birthplace, in the northwest corner of Panola Co.] in search of beare dogs. succeeded in getting too fine start dogs, we went out yesterday late in the evening started one at the back of our field & killed it, tell Caleb we got him up a tree about ½ mile south east of of [sic] the east end of Pennsylvania Avinew [a joke], it was then in the knight three miles from home and in a half Aire [hour] from there home. we could not strike our trail consequently we had to cut our way through to the open woods. we got home at ten Oclock last knight all well. we ran three [two words illegible here], we went again this morning & had 3 more chaces [chases] & killed two Clinton killed one & I killed one. Major Dickens was with us today the last race was after one of those that don't climb trees he was a whale, they are getting very saucy & catching hogs by the whole sale and even wallowing in my cotton field but [end of page] but I think these new dogs will make them sit farther. tel Caleb they are eaqual to Old Red and both young. tell Caleb also that Clintons three Pups is whales & they will make the bear set farther when they get grown. Mr Prince I have nothing of interest to wright as you have already seen but I thought Caleb might bee interested some in my hunting tale as he knows the ground and could appreciate a portion of it at least.

When Ike McCaslin goes into the wilderness to try to get his first look at Old Ben, he realizes after a time that even though he has left his gun behind he is still tainted by civilization. He must relinquish everything if he is to see the bear. He hangs his watch and compass on a bush, leans his snake stick beside them, and pushes on into the Big Bottom, which Faulkner described earlier as "the same solitude, the same loneliness through which frail and timorous man had merely passed without altering it, leaving no mark nor scar, which looked exactly as it must have looked when the first ancestor of Sam Fathers' Chickasaw predecessors crept into it and looked about him. . . ." Ike gets lost, comes upon the old bear's tracks, its imprint distinguished by the trap-maimed paw, and follows to where the bear is waiting, appropriately, beside the watch and compass. The boy and the bear study each other briefly across a small glade before the bear fades back into the wilderness to await its symbolic fate. The fate of the bear, of course, is the fate of the wilderness itself, for the bear, as Faulkner once suggested, is the spirit of that wilderness.

During the late 1880s word got around that the southern forests could be had for relatively low prices (most of the farmers regarded the timber as an obstacle), and speculators, usually from outside the South, came with a fury to buy up or lease large blocks of timber. By 1900 the sawmills in Mississippi had doubled, and four years later the state ranked third among lumber-producing states. In "Mississippi Forests," Nollie Hickman reports that in 1925 lumber output from these virgin forests reached an all-time high of slightly more than 3 billion board feet. For me the most dramatic illustration of how much timber all of this involves is found in old topographic maps that indicate woodland by green shading. Arrange them in a stack in chronological sequence—they are updated periodically—and flip through from past to present. You can read a good portion of the history of the area in terms of a steadily diminishing green shade.

As I have mentioned, my grandfather cut and milled timber in the Tallahatchie and Yocona Bottoms for many years. One of his smaller mills, called a groundhog mill, was along the route to the Stone camp, and I am confident that Faulkner and his fellow hunters knew of it. Like the wilderness, that mill has vanished. In fact, one of the large lumber companies in Memphis (not unlike the fictional Memphis lumber company to whom Major de Spain sells the timber rights in "The Bear") sent a representative to Panola with an offer to buy my grandfather's entire lumber business. My grandfather declined, and within a month his main sawmill and lumberyard containing thousands of board feet of prime hardwood lumber were nothing but ash. Not exactly like the big guns sent to kill McCabe when he refused to sell his brothel in Altman's movie *McCabe and Mrs. Miller*, but close. That is, my grandfather was not shot, but he never fully recovered financially from the fire, his business being uninsured.

I don't have the sense that my grandfather had available to him the assurances of protection from loss in the lumber business in Panola County—or that he would have availed himself of those assurances, given the probable cost. (It is not apples and oranges to note that General Stone lost virtually all of his land in Panola County, owing to the fact that he could not pay drainage taxes. Apparently he was not insured against losses in other ventures.) Before the mill fire my grandfather had another uninsured loss—a huge float of hardwood timber on the Tallahatchie River near Belmont above the hunting grounds. He didn't own a spur-line railroad, so his crew skidded the cut timber from the woods to the banks of the Tallahatchie and rolled log after log into the current. Downstream was a log boom that my grandfather and father had constructed, with the plan of catching the timber and then hauling it to their main sawmill nearby. As they waited at the boom, the Tallahatchie began to rise unexpectedly. There were no NOAA weather forecasts available or iPhones to alert you that the river was dangerously on the rise from flash-flooding upstream. My father said he looked up as the timber came around the bend of the Tallahatchie and the churn of foam created by the head logs of the float was like froth on a giant mad-dog's mouth. The timber broke through the boom and spread itself for miles downstream in the flood. Farmers later would pull their mule wagons up to my grandfather's sawmill with choice hardwood logs marked by metal die on one end with my grandfather's signature *S*. "Hey, Mr. Seay, can you mill this up for me?" Groan.

There was no strict evidence linking the Memphis lumber company with the fire, but one of the locals said that on the day before the fire he saw two Brazilians lingering on the Batesville town square. How he dreamed up the Brazilian identity—or thought he could distinguish a Brazilian from, say, a Bedouin or an Inuit—is a mystery. But local lore rules, and in that lore the story of hired Brazilians setting fire to my grandfather's mill and lumberyard is as firm as any in Faulkner's fiction.

The tract on which General Stone's camp was situated is currently listed in the Panola County property records as held in a revocable living trust by an owner who lives out of state. That person and other family members, some residing in Mississippi, have evidenced little interest in the Stone clubhouse except to the extent that profit could be had by selling its artifacts online. When I learned of the online offerings—doors, fireplace bricks, and the like—I was outraged that the clubhouse had been stripped bare. I could not countenance the thought that my home county would possibly be left without a visible trace of Faulkner's sojourns there. I flew to Mississippi from North Carolina and summoned the help of a friend in Batesville, Kenneth Brasell. We drove the sixty miles to New Albany, Mississippi, where a relative of the owner had the artifacts in his garage. I told the man I wanted to buy the whole lot. I do not know if he was sensitive in any appreciable way, prior to my visit and conversation with him, to the idea of provenance and how that might best be honored. I won't attempt here to parse the concept, pro or con, of private ownership of items invested with historical or literary significance. All I knew was that I wanted to ensure that each artifact found a habitation that would honor the connection with Faulkner's achievement, and in my mind it was fundamental that the first site should be in Panola, my home county and an indisputable corner of Yoknapatawpha.

After consulting with Kenneth, I made an offer and we bought all of the doors, some bricks, and a window frame with empty glass panels. Together we donated one door to our Batesville Public Library, and divided the remaining items. I donated one of my doors to the University of Mississippi Museum in Oxford. I am still looking for appropriate sites for the other door and the window frame.

The family apparently bought the land in order to put it in the federal wetlands program and collect money while the land reverts to whatever growth will establish itself. Fair enough, but I seriously doubt their dedication to ecology and anything but profit, given their advertising the artifacts of the clubhouse on eBay. Beaver dams now create flooding that has put the clubhouse, as I have noted, in a state of desuetude. My hope had always been to initiate restoration of the clubhouse in my retirement years and seek registration with the National Register of Historic Places. But by the time I learned of the family's stripping of the clubhouse and its flooding, it was too late for anything other than the recovery of those remnants I've described. I recently drove out Dummy Line Road—the foundation of which is the Dummy Line railroad that afforded Faulkner and his hunters access to General Stone's hunting camp and on which my father hauled a corpse back to town in his motor car when the world was covered in ice—and got as close to the site of the clubhouse as possible in a four-wheel-drive pickup with the idea of walking the remaining distance—as a trespasser, I assume—but the thick growth and briars and danger of cotton-mouth moccasins turned me back.

When I first discovered the clubhouse in the 1970s, I knelt down beside the artesian spring and cupped water in my hands to drink. Even then, after centuries of flow, the spring delivered a stream of water as thick as your wrist. The cold, deep earthiness of the water, with its tincture of sulfur, seemed to me an apt distillation of all that the land had borne, both the real Panola and its fictional corner in Faulkner's Yoknapatawpha. Old Ben's blood, Venus's blood, gunpowder, the spoor of Jim Hancock's white otter, Audubon's crayon, Sutpen's fury, the ash of my grandfather's mill, the last breath of General Stone's son in that same artesian spring, Major de Spain's ink on the lumber company's lease, the frail purchase of my father's motor-car wheels on the Dummy Line, the rumor of Brazilians, Faulkner's footsteps and shadow. It was all there, blent in an alchemy of dream.

After Old Ben has finally been hunted down and Major de Spain has sold the timber rights to the Memphis lumber company, Ike catches a ride on the log train at Hoke's and heads into the Big Bottom a final time, thinking along the way of what the train has come to mean:

> It had been harmless then. They would hear the passing log-train sometimes from the camp; sometimes, because nobody bothered to listen for it or not. . . . But it was different now. It was the same train, engine cars and caboose, even the same enginemen brakeman and conductor . . . yet this time it was as though the train (and not only the train but himself, not only his vision which had seen it and his memory which remembered it but his clothes too, as garments carry back into the clean edgeless blowing of air the lingering effluvium of a sick-room or of death) had brought with it into the doomed wilderness even before the actual axe the shadow and portent of the new mill not even finished yet and the rails and ties which were not even laid; and he knew now what he had known as soon as he saw Hoke's this morning but had not yet thought into words: why Major de Spain had not come back, and that after this time he himself, who had had to see it one time other, would return no more.

Big Boss Man

A load of travertine marble slabs had come in on a flatbed trailer, and it fell to me, as labor foreman, to get it unloaded. It was to be the façade of the entrance to the building we were constructing at the University of Mississippi, from the ground up. Travertine is the stone that architect Richard Meier used for the Getty. Lincoln Center is also clad in travertine. It has a long history in architecture. The Roman Colosseum is the largest building in the world to employ travertine. When I first looked at the slabs on the flatbed, I had only a scant notion of how I was going to get that colossal mass of stone safely to the ground.

This was in 1959, and there were no forklifts, no front-end loaders, no hydraulic anything on our job. Almost all our work was manual. In a worn and faded blue spiral notebook, I find a list that I took to the hardware store one day for replacement tools, owing to breakage or wear. All tools of manual labor.

Picks—short	4
Picks—w/ hoe end	3
Shovels—RH [round head]	6
Shovels—FH [flat head]	7
Shovels—sharpshooter	3
Files—6 in. triangular mill bastard	3

(The files were for our filer, who devoted his entire day to the sharpening of handsaws for the carpenters. He worked in a little tin shack that was moved from job to job.)

We had a cable-type buck hoist for lifting material to the upper stories, but it was stationary and of no use in unloading the marble. And so it was for me and my labor crew to somehow get the nearly milk-white travertine to the ground and stored safely. I was labor foreman not because I knew all that much about labor, but because I was a white boy and had had two years of college. None of that, though, was helping me figure out how to do what the construction supervisor had told me to do—get the stone unloaded and keep it up out of the mud. The truck driver was sitting in his cab, fuming to be unloaded and deadheading home.

The labor crew varied in number, anywhere from seventeen down to a dozen, some quitting, some laid off, depending on the construction schedule. The roster was composed primarily of Black men. The remaining four or five were white men, and they resented me almost to a man. With the Black workers I had somewhat better acceptance. But among them was the man who had me and my inexperience figured most precisely. Theo. Not a misnomer. He was an imposing figure, just over six feet in height, strongly built, hair graying around the temples, savvy, and a subtle way of resisting the authority of the white man, the racism of the day. And he knew that I was stymied in my attempt to get the travertine to the ground.

The men could not deadlift it off the trailer, for fear that they would harm themselves—and the marble—in the transfer. I had devised an incline to try to get it down efficiently and without danger—four-by-four timbers angled from trailer to ground, by which to slide the stone down, but the four-bys kept going askew. At the same time I had to see that the wooden pallets I had brought in would support and keep clean the few pieces we had managed to unload. While I was occupied with that, Theo—without consulting me—had the Black men in the crew cut two-by-fours at an angle to provide pointed ends. He then had them drive the stakes into the ground and nail them to the lower end of the four-bys to secure a purchase, which my engineering had failed to do. He tied the top ends to the trailer railing with baling wire. The crew got the stone to the ground, and I tried to regain some degree of authority by having them get the travertine to my pallets and cover it with plastic sheeting.

What followed from this was that Theo and I formed an unspoken agreement. He knew that I knew what had occurred, and I knew that to continue as labor foreman I needed to recognize his authority. No need to verbalize. Afterward I would lay out the projects for the day and leave it to him to accomplish them. He led the Black crew to that end—I can't say that he did it unobtrusively—and I signaled for the white crew to follow. They did not like this, but they needed work. And I was the big boss man.

MILLER WAS SQUATTING beside a propane burner melting lead in a small crucible when I arrived unannounced at the construction site one Saturday to check on some elevations that we needed for plans in building a retaining wall on Monday. Miller had cut the conical tips from a dozen or so paper Dixie cups and placed the tips in roughly similar depressions he had formed in the ground. After glancing up at me briefly, and without a word, he turned back to his make-do assembly line. He was making lead weights for his trot lines on the Yocona River (Faulkner's Yoknapatawpha River) near his trailer. When he poured the molten lead into the paper tips, the paper ignited but held long enough for the lead to assume the shape of weights, though not as smooth and free of pocks as those available in bait shops. The eyes for receiving the trot line were fashioned from pieces of wire he had cut and bent, then inserted upright into the center of the paper tips before pouring the lead.

Miller was guessing that he could come in on a Saturday, take what he needed from the plumbers' shed, make his weights, and get out undetected. The burner and crucible would have cooled by the time the plumbers returned to work on Monday. And they were not likely to notice the relatively small foray into their lead supply. Otherwise they would have been pissed. Had Miller asked, they would have said yeah sure take some lead, use the burner, bring us some catfish. But that was not Miller's way. He was getting back at whatever it was, unnamed and unrealized, that had left him dispossessed, unhoused, in life. A void that he would never fill. Stealing, dissembling, making trouble, whatever path he could find, straight or crooked. He was short in stature, wiry, fixed, quick as a snake.

He knew that I knew what he was doing, and he didn't care. He didn't care because he knew that I knew he would somehow get back at me if I reported him. I had learned something of his ways when I worked with him on Lynn Dodson's steel crew before I became labor foreman. I had some creds there—pulled from the common labor crew and elevated to rod-buster by Lynn, a highly regarded foreman, to work with his crew laying reinforcing steel for floor slabs and later erecting structural steel. But the shared status of steel crew membership—rod-busters, beam-walkers—and the work companionship went only so far in Miller's economy. If it went anywhere at all.

Before the structural steel part of the construction, we put coils of wire crosswise over our shoulders and bent to the steel reinforcing rods—rebars—to secure them in a grid with wire and pliers before the concrete was poured for floor slabs. The rebar provides additional tensile strength to the concrete. Today rebar is typically secured by tie-wire twisters and standard cuts of wire that are looped under the rebar and pulled upward, making for a uniform twist. There are also fancy automatic rebar-connecting guns. And there are forklifts, front-end loaders, Bobcats for small earthmoving projects, hydraulic equipment everywhere you look on construction sites. For the most part we had only picks and shovels, handsaws, pliers, coils of wire that we learned not to leave out overnight lest it rust or get so hot in the morning sun that it gave us a start when we looped it over our bare shoulders.

We did, however, have the use of a crane contracted from the structural steel company to lift the steel into place. (The crane was not available at the time I was overseeing the unloading of the travertine.) For the structural steel erection, Lynn teamed me up with Miller. We shimmed columns and straddled crossbeams, working our way along like cautious raccoons until we got up the nerve to walk the beams. We had spud wrenches, nuts, bolts, and washers for bolting the steel in place once the crane operator had lifted it to us. (Hot rivets—such as those being tossed, white hot, from forger with tongs to riveter with metal bucket in the Empire State Building section of Ric Burns's film *New York*—had been replaced by nuts and bolts.)

Each column and beam had four holes in the plies where the two pieces of steel were to be joined, horizontal beam to upright column. We worked the tapered end of a spud wrench into one of the holes, jimmied it back and forth in order to bring the holes of the column and the beam into alignment, inserted a bolt into one of the free holes, placed a washer on the bolt, then the nut, and torqued it snug tight.

One day Miller and I were working a column and crossbeam. I was astraddle the beam, and Miller had a ladder up the column. We had secured the other end of the beam to its column. As I leaned over to insert the bolt, Miller pulled the spud wrench from the hole he had chosen for alignment. The freed beam slipped down a few inches but was caught at an angle on the column. Forgetting that the crane cable was still attached to the beam for safety, I was seized with a paralyzing fear that the beam weight combined with my weight would push the column slightly outward enough for the beam to slip farther and break away from its hold on the opposite end.

The image lodged in my memory is of Miller's eyes and the particular set of his lips as he looked up at me. It sounds melodramatic, I realize, but I can never be sure whether it was Miller's sense of a joke to pull the spud wrench, knowing the beam would slip downward and give me a scare, or whether it was a threat for my future reference.

I backed off the end of the beam enough to where he could refit his spud wrench, and we completed the work. Later when I had come down from the beam, the sight of another crane that the steel company had left temporarily on the job site caught my eye. Suspended midair from its cable was a welding machine they had been using to reconnect some steel end plates they had miscalculated. It was mounted on a set of wheels, and in order to protect it from theft, it was kept aloft while they were away. I went up to Miller, now descended from his ladder, and pointing to the welding machine, I said, "That's your heart, Miller, suspended. And it's not coming down." Part of my declaration was the college boy who had read some poetry and understood metaphor.

Miller looked at me half quizzically. I think he more or less got the import of what I was saying, but then he formed a twisted smile that told me he had no regrets or apologies. His blue eyes were the eyes of every Nazi stereotype you've seen in war movies. A cliché, but nonetheless profoundly unsettling. In a time warp, Miller would have been at Charlottesville with a Tiki Torch and a baseball bat.

THE DAY-TO-DAY jesting that is standard in most workplaces is usually predictable and lacking in traction. One of the Black workers on the labor crew was not afflicted with that ordinariness, though, and he rarely failed to amuse us with his antics and jestful spirit. His name was James Williams, but he insisted that we call him Samson. He was born with what he called a "bail" over his head, and he claimed that it gave him special powers, including strength. What he meant was "veil," but he had a slight speech impediment. It is quite possible that the impediment figured somehow in my amusement. I was not free of the way some of us as youths found humor in impediments among schoolmates—and allowed that cruelty to inform part of our sense of humor. It can take a lifetime to realize the wrong of that taunting, and for some the realization is never gained, nor is it attempted. I never laughed at Samson's impeded speech in and of itself. I did, however, laugh at his improvisations that included speech and were consciously designed to elicit laughter, though not by way of his articulation.

What amused me foremost was the way he presented himself as a kind of court jester of the construction site and at the same time tried to live up to his self-assigned nickname. He was indeed quite strong, and I could always count on him to bear more than his share of the load. Those loads were usually serious business. No fooling around or someone could get hurt. Occasionally, though, Samson made a mock-heroic show of taking the heavy end of whatever—a flanged culvert, an uneven stack of sheet metal, anything—or simply stepping in and hoisting it by himself. He was his own Samson, and with no shorn locks. His show was funny—and often endearing, but that was not a term I would utter on the job site.

Legend has it that to be born *en caul*—a fragment of the amniotic membrane covering the head like a veil—is to possess special powers. Lord Byron was born with a caul, as was Freud. So too was Liberace. I told Samson that a person in a book I had read was born with a veil (I used Samson's term rather than caul) and he was protected from drowning. I knew not to let the college boy out of his cage, so I did not name David Copperfield, nor did I tell Samson that young David's veil was sold in a raffle, for fear that he, Samson, would begin brooding over the whereabouts of his own veil, the source of his special powers. After he nodded that he understood his good standing—the agency of the veil with a person in a book—I told him again that he was safe from drowning. He said it was a good thing because he couldn't swim a lick.

When I had a two-man project that required my having a hand in, I always chose Samson as my partner. While he was sometimes the clown and a source of amusement, I chose him primarily because he was a willing worker. These two-man projects usually involved weekend work, when my time was not occupied with overseeing the labor crew. Samson welcomed the weekend work, for it paid time and a half for work beyond the standard forty hours a week.

One particular project I remember in detail, because I screwed it up superbly. A bulldozer had been contracted to come in on a Saturday to move earth off several hills in order to reduce the amount of manual shovel work in laying a section of concrete culverts for drainage, scheduled for Monday. The construction supervisor had given me a rudimentary lesson in the use of a transit for determining the elevations of the area where the dozer was to work. A transit is an optical instrument with a built-in spirit level mounted on a tripod. The transit has to be leveled before reading elevations. Samson was my rodman, holding the grade rod upright, imperial gradations on one side, metric on the other. We used the imperials, feet and inches, true to the blueprints.

I won't list chapter and verse, but I failed to level the transit properly. Not that it is neurosurgery, but if one is unfamiliar with transit work—setting up the tripod securely on uneven ground, leveling the transit with the spirit level, taking accurate readings off the grade rod, calculating necessary grade—it is easy for things to go awry. We were working with the dozer operator, me at my position with the transit, Samson moving back and forth with the grade rod. Today the communication would be by wireless, but I had only hand signals to tell the dozer operator what degree of earth to grade. Samson would run over near the dozer with the rod, I would take a reading, Samson would run back a safe distance, I would give my hand signal, and the dozer would plow into the earth. All very hectic, not least because the dozer operator was like the truck driver with the travertine. He wanted to be done with this stop-and-go stuff and join up with his buddies drinking beer on a Saturday afternoon. Typically the reading of elevations would be done beforehand, with stakes driven in the ground and crayoned to tell the operator how much to grade. Makes for a more seamless operation. A clean tool makes a happy worker.

Added to this disorder was Samson's inattention to the side of the rod he faced toward me. Midway through a reading, I would realize I was seeing metric gradations and have to shout to him to turn the rod around to the imperial. He couldn't hear me at first, so he had to come over to learn what I was shouting. The dozer operator sat there, revving the engine up and down.

The upshot of all this was that on Monday we—or rather my supervisor—discovered that huge amounts of earth had to be trenched through by shovel, owing to my skewed transit, Samson's double-dealing rod, and the dozer operator's impatience.

Associated with that section involving concrete culverts was another section at the bottom of a hill requiring a drainage system. The delivery truck with the culverts could not access the area, so we had to unload the culverts at the top of the hill. The challenge was to get the culverts down the hill to where we would do the trenching and installation. My supervision of the bulldozer grading had been a comedy of errors, but there was nothing funny about it to the construction supervisor. I was very much out of favor at the time of the hilltop challenge. He let me know that those culverts had better arrive at the bottom of the hill intact and lined up ready to install. And that I better have a plan in mind for getting the job done quickly; we were running behind schedule. Also to let me know that his confidence in me was waning, he said he would be checking the culvert joints personally before the inspector came, so the hemp joint-packing better be tamped in tight and not show-ing through the cement mortar around the joint.

To emphasize further his dwindling confidence in his labor foreman's know-how, he had the carpenters construct a wooden chute down the hill—a forty- to fifty-foot drop at around forty-five degrees. He instructed them to use scrap plywood and then mop oil on it. The idea being that the lubrication would ease the downward slide of the culverts. Because the supervisor gave me the orders directly, I could not delegate the project to Theo. But perhaps I should have. The supervisor's idea that the oil application would facilitate things was way off mark. The culverts would not slide by their own weight, so I had to put a man on either side of the chute to push and pull, in effect wrestling the culverts down. That effort was too slow, too tedious, and I was beginning to panic.

That is when Samson stepped up in full visionary mode, empowered by his birth veil, seeing the world as I could not. He proposed that we roll the culverts down the hill, alternating the flanged end each time. The culverts would roll in favor of the flange; one culvert would roll one way, the next one the other way. He and a fellow worker, Henry Cook, would be at the bottom of the hill to push them off to the side before the next one came rolling down. Two groups of culverts, safe and out of the path of the next culvert.

Samson's plan was working fine until one of the workers went to a culvert that was lying at a distance outside the main grouping and gave it a push off the hill—thinking, I guess, that he could save us time by not bringing the culvert to the launching area. Or not thinking at all. Added to that, he pointed the flange in the same direction as the previous one. Samson saw what was happening and rushed forward to stop the rogue culvert. He later said he was going to tackle it. Tackle it he tried, but the culvert, which was over knee-high, flung him in the air like a piece of fluff. And then careened into its unintended mates. From the top of the hill, it looked like a minor banzai attack, several of the frontline culverts in shatters. I knew what the supervisor was going to say—and he did: Why did I not use the chute he had the carpenters make? And, short of that, why was I not watching each culvert as it was placed for release? I had a reasonable answer for the first question, but not for the second.

Before the disaster Theo was irked that Samson had come up with the alternating flange plan and had gotten my attention before he, Theo, could have a say. I could see it in his bearing and avoidance of eye contact. But the shambles at the foot of the hill changed his affect remarkably. Schadenfreude. Theo made sure that the supervisor saw him shake his head as though he could not believe the idiocy of what he saw at the foot of the hill.

AS I MENTIONED EARLIER, Theo had a subtle way of resisting the racism of the day. But that resistance had limits that were clear to him, and so he had developed a cunning that enabled him to skirt the danger of transgression, whose rules had been codified by whites. Remember that this was a time and place in which three years earlier the Black youth Emmett Till, after false claims by a white woman, was murdered by whites in Money, Mississippi, only seventy-six miles from Oxford, the location of our construction site. A time and place also in which three years later there would be rioting at the University of Mississippi when James Meredith entered as the first Black student. Two men were killed by gunshots, cars burned, and property destroyed. None of this is to suggest that there was racial strife among our workers. At least not overtly so. And that was owing to the fact that the Black construction workers, willingly or not, played the hand they were dealt by the culture. Except for Theo. He was not insolent, but his manner told you that he operated at a certain remove. For instance he did not invite any exchange of humor with the whites.

I never heard the Black workers referred to in racist terms on the job site, but apart from the work they did side by side with the whites on the labor crew, they kept to themselves during breaks and lunch time. Usually these were uneventful times, but on Fridays at noon during football season there was a female student who would come to her dormitory window, within view of our job site, and bare her breasts. Getting worked up for the football weekend, I guess. The white workers, from their lunch-time perch, would hoot and holler, encouraging her to show more. The Black workers, sitting in an area apart, were silent, usually looking away. Samson would look up briefly and then turn back to the ham biscuit that someone, mostly likely his mother, had put in his lunch pail. Theo's countenance changed to that of unmistakable scorn, and he turned his back on the young woman's display. He would not be toyed with.

In this same context, another contrast existed between the two groups of workers. One of the white workers, upon learning that the flanged end of a culvert was called the female end, went over during lunch break and dry-humped a culvert for the amusement of his fellow white workers. The irony was that it was the male end. In his defense, I should note that the female end was against an embankment. Then again, maybe it didn't matter. The Black workers never behaved in this way on the job site. Probably because at some level they were aware of how that kind of behavior could cast them in a role associated with the myth of sexually predatory Black men. That is not to say that there was no randiness in their part of town across the tracks. I'm sure there was, no question, but in my view, they were saints in the realm of public dry-humping.

It would be a misrepresentation, and trite, to present these workers, Black and white, in simplistic contrast to each other. Not that I would try to present the Black workers as having a corner on dignity and long suffering. They were capable of the same dithering, pettiness, and wheedling as the white workers. The two were equal in flaws and equal in having to bear the consequences of those flaws. The heartbreaking difference, though, is that the Black workers had the added burden of living at a severe and unjust disadvantage in the culture they were born into.

In taking leave of these workers, I want to cast a light more favorable to their better angels. His anger and aggression toward the world notwithstanding, Miller was struggling to feed his family, saving three dollars on lead weights for his trot lines and bringing home catfish. Theo was inventing a way to preserve his dignity and sense of worth in the face of grinding odds. As for the lunchtime comedian, the light dims a lumen or two. But one could do worse than dry-hump a concrete pipe. Though not needing his angels illuminated, Samson should be included here to brighten further his story of a veil that gave him strength and a vision of how he wanted the world to be. As for myself, I had the plan of returning someday to college. Which I did. (I had dropped out of college to help my family following an accident that left my father immobilized, but that is another story.) Ironically my reentry several years later was at this very university where I helped build a classroom building from the ground up.

I cannot claim that I learned more on the construction site than in any classroom I ever sat in. There were fundamental differences, to be sure, and there is appeal in the notion that the lessons of on-the-ground experience make for a sure hand on the wheel and an uncluttered agenda, whereas the lessons of academic toil have strong potential for abstracting too much and creating a maze of competing options. Either way, when seeking to know something, to do it the right way, there is always some truth that is elusive, fugitive. And sometimes a veil through which, improbably, we are given vision.

The Chandeliers

That is what Glyn, our pilot and fishing guide, called the Chandeleurs. The Chandeliers. A small chain of barrier islands in the Gulf of Mexico, beginning some thirty-five miles from the airport in Gulfport, Mississippi, and extending another fifty miles or so into the Gulf. For the ducal sum of twenty-five dollars per person he was flying us to Errol Island, one of the South Chandeleur Islands. This was in 1969. We had booked the charter, which included lodging and food, with his company, B-Line Flying Service. The loaves of Wonder Bread in the bags beside me in the rear of the little Cessna suggested there was probably sliced bologna in the coolers and we should rig up as soon as we landed and wade out to cast for dinner.

To get the first three of our party of six, our gear, and two Igloo coolers of ice out to his Chandeliers, Glyn had taken the rear seats out of the plane. I was seated on one of the Igloos. There was no seat belt, but I was too keyed up to care. Despite the Wonder Bread,

I envisioned a sea-weathered cabin—something redolent of vintage fishing camps. Maybe a palm tree or two marking a landing strip of crushed shell or some such. All in the service of a weekend of dedicated surf fishing.

When we were barely free of the runway and over the Gulf, the stall buzzer went off. The aerodynamics elude me, but to judge from what I've read, it was not solely an issue of weight. Glyn's angle of attack, as it is called by pilots, was off. He quickly lowered the nose of the Cessna and got enough speed to level us out and get the right angle of attack. Then I noticed on the instrument panel that the oil gauge was twitching back and forth. I asked Glyn what that meant, and he said not to worry, that he had worked on the engine the day before. And that the Chandeliers weren't far off, we'd be there soon.

I think the voicing of the word appealed to Glyn, though it may also have been a matter of local appellation. The Chandeliers. Whatever, he was pretty well on the mark. The Chandeleurs were christened by explorer Pierre Le Moyne d'Iberville when he anchored there on February 1, 1700, eve of La Fête de la Chandeleur. Candlemas, when candles to be used in religious ceremonies during the year are blessed. Candle Mass, Chandeleurs, Chandeliers, lighting both sacred and secular.

By figurative association with Candlemas, the three Chandeleur lighthouses that once stood—successively, each one downed by storms—were likened to giant candles. The final one toppled into the sea after Katrina in 2005.

Errol Island, to which Glyn was flying us, was only a speck on US Geological Survey maps at the time of our trip in 1969, but it no longer appears on the maps, or at least not on the October 2005 map, following Katrina. It is my guess that it is now completely submerged. There are, however, fishing charters today to some of the Chandeleurs. Of which, more later.

On our approach to Errol Island, Glyn took a low sweep over it. We could see sharks below working the clear water. Glyn said not to worry, they were either sand sharks or blacktips and would be interested only in the fish that we would be towing behind us on long stringers buoyed by Styrofoam floats. I did not see the crushed-shell landing strip that I had envisioned, and I realized that Glyn was doing low-level reconnaissance to determine if anything—logs, crab traps, derelict boats—had washed up on the beach during the last storm, requiring that he find somewhere else to land.

We were clear and made a smooth landing, then taxied up to the cabin where we would lodge for the weekend. It was sea-weathered, for sure, but dignified only in the sense that it appeared to have withstood more storms than it was built for. Mostly it was scrap plywood, rusted tin roofing, and open-air ventilation. The sheets of plywood were multicolored, their placement governed more or less by color grouping. Green, blue, yellow, and unpainted. Nailed here and there to cover holes were strips of plastic tarp fluttering in the breeze.

When Glyn unloaded us and our gear, he returned to the mainland to fetch the other three members of our party. The Igloos remained in the plane, seats for two. Probably he did not want to spend time at the airport replacing the regular seats. And later he would need the coolers aboard to take home whatever was left of the catch after our dinners. We had planned to begin fishing as soon as we landed and got sorted out, but we realized that we did not know how to prepare and deploy the stringers and floats that would keep our catch at a safe distance from us. Glyn had left us some beer, so we sat in the sand and looked out over the surf, talking about whatever guys talk about when they are lifted from their routines and set down on a strand surrounded by softly dazzling water.

When Glyn returned, there was just enough time for us to rig up and wade out into the surf before dark, the stringers and floats trailing behind us like large lures. Glyn had given us very quick instructions in their use. The sharks were taken up with a school of bait fish in the distance, to judge from the fretted water, and in the short time we had before dusk we got tight with enough fish for dinner. Speckled sea trout, or specks. Sleek, feisty, caught to eat.

Almost all my fishing now is catch-and-release. In 2007 my friend Will invited me to join him in Montana for fly-fishing. I was addicted from the get-go. There is deep pleasure in releasing a landed fish, seeing it disappear back into its mystical element. There is also deep pleasure in eating a fish fresh from the water. The freshest I've ever had was in Mexico, fishing out of Zihuata-nejo. A Pacific yellowtail, prepared two hours after catch. The boat captain pulled into an island cove with a thatched roof restaurant, where they made ceviche with some of the yellowtail and grilled the remainder. Foodwise, fishwise, I was ruint ever after, seeking the match of that fish fresh out of the sea.

We cast for redfish along some shoals off Errol Island the next day, with no success. So we went back to the surf in front of the cabin and began catching specks with regularity. You can cast a Kastmaster lure a country mile, and we were able to get out to where the specks were working. They whittled away the bucktails we had attached to the Kastmasters, but that gave us brief spells to attach fresh ones and string up any recent catch.

I had been assigned one of the stringers. Glyn had instructed us in the use of a particular slip knot for quick release in case a shark hit. Fishing from about forty feet offshore, I felt a purposeful tug and was jerked around, my back now to the Gulf. A friend shouted for me to release the knot. I reached behind me and found a hard knot. In his eagerness to string a speck, one of our members had retied the stringer but neglected the slip knot. Normally the stringer was attached to one's belt. Providence had it that our man put it in my rear belt loop, and I was able to rip it loose. Watching the Styrofoam float make erratic progress into the Gulf, I waded to shore and took a long break for a beer.

That night we sat under a wing of the Cessna, eating trout that Glyn had fried on his propane stove. It wasn't raining, but we were drawn to the underwing to sit in the sand and eat our fish. It was partly a respite from the dreary cabin. Mainly though I think the shelter of the wing gave a faint sense of security—and para-doxically an openness to the night around us. There was a breeze off the water and a quiet surf. The wing's shadow enhanced the moonlight; occasionally a shooting star added its quiet drama. We talked about our wives and girlfriends, our children, the ups and downs of work. For reasons I am unsure of, there was little or no talk of sex. We talked also about the day's fishing, but that gave over to tales of fish we had lost in the past.

I recalled a fish I hooked in the Florida Keys—a permit, which is a stubborn fish, easily spooked, and a long runner on the flats. Between Man Key and Woman Key. Uncanny. This was before I took up fly-fishing, so I was using a spinning rig. My guide and I spotted the permit tailing at a distance, and the guide was able to pole our boat to within casting distance. As luck would have it, I placed a live crab out in front of the permit, and the fish took it. The fish quickly ran out over half the line of my spool, so the guide cranked the motor to follow and close some of the distance. After about twenty or thirty taut minutes of playing the fish, I felt the line suddenly go slack. My guide, a young man with whom I had good rapport, shouted at me. "You horsed it!" Meaning that, in his estimation, I had hauled back too strongly when I should have let the fish continue to run. I have contradicted a guide only twice in my fishing days, and this was one of the times. "I did not horse that fish!" Then we looked at each other and started laughing. And commiserating. I did not horse that fish.

Early the next day a plane swooped over our beach and dropped a small parachute with a canister attached. Glyn retrieved it, pulled out a note, and ran to his plane, yelling that his son had had a heart attack. We watched the Cessna fade into the distance and looked at each other in dismay, not knowing anything but that we were not now our provisioner's main concern and we were on an island in the Gulf of Mexico without any means of communication.

Thinking back on that moment and the anxiety of isolation, I am reminded of the movie *Wind River*. The FBI agent Jane, in a tense moment, asks the Native American reservation sheriff Ben, "Shouldn't we just maybe wait for backup?" Ben replies, "This isn't the land of waiting for backup, Jane. This is the land of you're on your own."

But our man Glyn did return. He said we needed to break camp and head for the mainland. I do not know how his son fared, but Glyn got us back safely, no stalls, no twitching oil gauge.

As it turns out, that Cessna is still in service. On a photo I took of the plane in front of our ramshackle cabin, I identified the N-number, N8422Z, and went to a Federal Aviation Administration database. The plane is registered to Bisti Aviation, and owner Donald Sitta, in Farmington, New Mexico. I was able to reach Don by phone. A Vietnam veteran and former commercial pilot, he has restored the Cessna to prime condition. On a CD from the FAA that lists the previous owners, he was able to trace the Cessna back to our Chandelier pilot and fishing guide Glyn Porter, owner 1966–69. The plane had once been stationed on a ranch near Marfa, Texas, that was so big the owner needed a plane for overseeing; it had also had owners in Fayetteville, Georgia; in Gainesville, Florida; and at a foundry in Texas, among others. It was first owned, in 1966, by Delta Aero Service, Greenville, Mississippi. It now has 9,000 hours on it. Don named it *Dirty Bird*:

> Jim, When I purchased the aircraft, I found there were many dirty corners (metaphorically & literally) that needed attention. Open up an inspection plate on the wing and it was long term dirty. Every place you looked it was the same. What a dirty airplane. At that time (mid 90's) there was a TV advertisement that featured some pigeons flying around looking for something nice to crap on. One of the pigeons was named Dirty Bird.

To learn of the current fishing situation in the Chandeleurs, I picked a charter service online, Due South Charters, Biloxi, Mississippi, and called them. The owner, Greg Thornton, said indeed he ran out to the Chandeleurs regularly, but does not camp out—rather the anglers have his mothership for lodging. When I told him of my experience in the Chandeleurs, I mentioned flying out there with Glyn Porter. Greg said, wait a minute, realizing that when he was a kid he once flew out there with his father and Glyn. Same plane. The image that had registered most forcefully on him was that of sharks in the water below.

I told him of my experience with the stringer and the shark. He said anglers came to his charter with all kinds of stringer rigs, but he was against most of them, especially a net bag sometimes called a do-net. But the do-net has its online advocates. In answer to an inquiry as to where one might obtain one, a respondent, Bob (aka E-Man), replies:

> There is a model call the do-net available at acadamey and other outlets. styrofoam ring w/ net bag. works great.
>
> Tip that may save your life!!! find and purchase an extra ring. take the bag off the first ring and use cable ties to join the 2 rings together. replace the net bag. use a 5' or less rope to tie this to your belt. IF YOU WOULD HAPPEN TO GET CAUGHT IN A RIP TIDE IN THE SURF YOU CAN DROP YOUR ROD AND REEL AND LAY ACROSS THE TOP OF YOUR DO-NET, W/ 2 RINGS IT WILL FLOAT YOU.
>
> bob

E-Man Bob was keen on the rip tide danger but did not say what to do if a shark takes your do-net. For my part, I arrived back in Gulfport undrowned and fully limbed, perched on an Igloo full of speckled trout and unopened packages of sliced bologna. Back in the land of backup.

The Single-Wide Wars

The only trailers we could lease on our budget, we discovered, were repos. Not exactly Airstream styling. Repo agents usually go to repossess a trailer during the morning when the defaulters are at work, or looking for work. The agents cut the tie-downs, disconnect utilities, and haul the trailers away. By and large the interiors of the trailers that are for lease are in the condition in which they were left on the morning before repossession. The matter of personal property such as furniture in a repossessed trailer is legally complicated, but it is moot here because the repos my then-wife and I looked at were devoid of furniture and other personal items—except for grease-laden skillets in the sinks, cinnamon bun wrappers, and empty bottles of Taaka vodka. The day was wicked hot, and the trailers on the asphalt lot were unventilated. Giving in to the heat, we settled for a single-wide that still had Christmas decorations in the windows.

There was a hole in the kitchen floor, but the floor had been covered by linoleum. A depression marked where the hole was. The business owner J. D., from whom we leased the single-wide, said walk around it. Which is what we learned to do. The hole was about six inches in diameter, no known provenance. Otherwise the kitchen was pretty well what you would expect in a fourteen-by-seventy-foot single-wide. Tight space, small appliances, small cabinets, small sink, small window over sink. In total the single-wide was 880 square feet. Probably about the size of Gatsby's closet.

On one end of the single-wide was a bedroom which we used as a study. The bay window gave onto a view of the magnolia I had planted on Christmas Day and named Christmas Belle, for my mother Lucie Belle. On the other end was the master bedroom and a view of Neville Creek, the centerline of which was the back boundary of our property. Above the bed was a ceiling fan that was about a foot above the head of anyone who raised to their knees. Between the two end rooms was a bath, the kitchen with a hole in the floor, and a dining/living area, where we lived and dined in the midst of the turmoil that followed our settling there in the single-wide.

We had bought two contiguous two-acre lots outright. After that expense, we could not afford two loans—the mortgage loan on our house in town and the construction loan for the house our architect had designed—so we decided to sell the house in town and lease a trailer to put on our four acres during construction. Plus I wanted to be on the land to learn its character—its terroir, so to speak—and watch the play of different seasons, especially in the tulip poplars along the creek.

To make sure that there were no restrictive covenants prohibiting a mobile home on the land, I had gone to the register of deeds at the county courthouse. I could find no applicable restrictions in the most recent Declaration of Restrictions, and so we went with confidence to a local trailer lot to choose our home for what would be the next fifteen months. (Several years later, however, while researching a matter regarding county codes—and after the single-wide had long since been taken back to J. D.'s lot—I found an entry in an earlier declaration restricting use of the land to permanent houses. But things had gone unchallenged initially, and we had lived under the impression that our single-wide bore the full armor of the law.)

Wars small and large are fought over borders, appurtenances, and treasury within. Our wars gravitated between small and large and involved all three particulars. They began as Wikipedia suggests they would: "The arrival of mobile homes in an area tend[s] to be regarded with alarm. . . ." Meaning that folks in stick-built houses with well-kept lawns don't want to see a single-wide being hauled onto the land next door. You can't fault that, especially if the single-wide is a beat-up dull gray with a V-shaped bay window on one end. And the haulers, in trying to make a sharp turn off the road, hauling seventy feet of dreadfulness, have knocked down a small specimen tree on a neighbor's land.

I realized later that the perfect tableau for the entire fifteen-month conflict and series of misunderstandings was the scene on the day I was sitting in the grass in front of the new house with Mr. Bowden and Toy Cheek. Bowden was always Mr. Bowden to me when I spoke to him. He was the retired farmer who had sold us the land the house was on. Cranky and opinionated, he felt that he held sway over all the land along the road that was named for him. He still had lots for sale up the hill from us. Toy Cheek I also addressed as Mister, Mr. Cheek, though I thought of him as Toy. The lasting—and eminently winning—impression I have of him is his taking up a handful of raked hay one day and bringing it to his nose, testing its readiness for baling. I had given permission to him and Bowden to cut the grass on our land and bale it for cattle that they owned together. He always struck me as a gentle man, and I don't think he knew the full subtext of the visit on which he was accompanying Bowden.

Ostensibly they were paying a neighborly visit, a kind of outdoor housewarming, but the real reason for the visit was for Bowden to express his displeasure with where the house was situated. Already he had an animus toward me for having moved the single-wide on the land. Among other reasons, he was siding with a disgruntled neighbor who had also bought land from him and built on it just before the single-wide's arrival. Someone had told Bowden that the single-wide devalued all the houses and land values in the neighborhood. No matter that I had explained to any and all that the single-wide was temporary and that we were following the architect's guidance.

The architect had situated the house along the boundary with that neighbor in order to allow for the space required for a septic field—and to take advantage of the slope of a hill—in addition to keeping the well at a required distance from the septic field. In dowsing with a dogwood limb, the contractor had found only a limited area to drill for water. And too the architect said that the plan would allow us to use the same septic system and water supply for the finished house, which would be close to where the single-wide was. Just a matter of switching over. It also afforded a sweeping view of the four acres.

After a few attempts at his version of civility, Bowden let go with his opinion of things. "Your house shouldn't be over there jam up on the boundary with that neighbor," he said, "houses ought to be in the middle of a lot." I was caught between indignation and a conscious need to try to shift the tenor. Then I remembered a humorous adage that I thought would meet the moment. "Opinions," I told Bowden, "are like ass holes; everybody has one but they're all different."

Wrong gambit. Bowden thought I was calling him an asshole. Toy picked up on my intent and said a few words aimed at détente. He managed to get Bowden headed back home, and later would give me a grin and hearty wave when he came by on his tractor. Bowden never got the imagined insult out of his craw. I tried to be a good neighbor, buy tomatoes from his vegetable stand in the summer, ask his advice on what kind of weed it was that I was having trouble with, and so on. Once I even called to let him know that one of his beef cattle was loose on my land, and I helped him

The Single-Wide Wars

round it up. But he carried his misinterpretation to the grave. No way you can explain to his kind the intended humor of ass holes, of which we all have one, along with a different opinion.

On another front I was trying to ward off the blitz of an alcoholic neighbor. He was relatively comfortable on his land until the single-wide appeared, and I say relatively because two houses had just been built on the hill above, compromising his view of sunsets. Still and all, he seemed peaceful enough sitting in his lawn chair with his wine, watching the setting sun. But he was primed for anger. It erupted when my driveway was cut, a gash in the red clay dirt along the boundary of his land, curving to our building site. Owing to heavy rain, the contractors could not lay the crushed stone surface for a week, so there was the red gash outside his window, magnified in the lens of wine and rage.

After the crushed stone was laid, he came striding across my land to confront me as I was inspecting the new driveway. He was going to report me to the county, he said, for impervious surface violation. (Impervious surface codes are intended to control the amount of runoff into adjoining waterways leading into the town's water reservoir.) He added that the driveway was unbearably ugly. The latter impression was what had thrown him into a rage; he did not care about impervious surface any more than I cared about split infinitives. I told him that the four acres carried an impervious surface allowance that the house and driveway would be well within, and that I wanted him present when the county agent came to measure. His wife convinced him to refrain from calling the county.

This man had a varied past. He was a retired lawyer who once served as mayor of a town on San Francisco Bay in the late 1960s and who included gonzo journalist Hunter S. Thompson among his friends. He died in Thailand. In the intervening years he became an alcoholic. While he could be very charming in his sober moments, he was a greed head and miser at heart. Once early in the morning I found him on my side of the fence that I was having constructed on our mutual border. The fence builders had left sections of four-by-four posts on the ground, along with remnants of two-by-six railing, and he was gathering all of it. I told him that the fence builders might have plans for the lumber as they continued work. He said that he had already gathered some the day before for kindling and firewood. Not a good idea, I told him, there was arsenic in the wood preservative. He said "hmm," and told me he had noticed that he got woozy when he built a fire the day before.

As for boundaries, he enjoyed an easement allowing him to keep a portion of his driveway that encroached on my land. At one point in the surveying of my property and arrangements for the loan, his initial easement got tangled up legally, and he announced that regardless he could sue me under the adverse possession principle, owing to the long length of time that he had used the driveway. Sort of like squatter's rights. I told him that I just wanted to keep the peace, please have his lawyer draw up another document and I would happily sign it. For some reason his lawyer failed to enter the plea before a deadline or some such, and he reiterated that he could still sue. I told him that I would have my lawyer prepare a document.

Which I did, but I failed to read the fine print in the deed of easement. There is a standard three-word phrase, *and to assigns*, used in documents drafted to cure (another legal term) an encroachment. The easement is made to so and so—*and to assigns*. Which means that he, FedEx trucks, anyone, including future *assigns*, could drive on my land in perpetuity. All because years prior, when he and his wife were the sole occupants of that and surrounding acreage, he failed to observe boundaries and laid his driveway as he pleased. It is my guess that that impulse was ultimately in the service of avarice. And was congenital.

When I informed him that I was having the fence put up around my land, he told me that a particular dogwood was on his side of the boundary and the fence should be built accordingly. I had the land resurveyed to establish a line for the fence contractors. The survey made clear that the dogwood was on my side of the boundary, and I told him of this. He nodded and walked away.

The Single-Wide Wars

The next family to occupy the house of the alcoholic were wonderful neighbors—the man a newscaster, his wife a home-maker, two daughters nothing but sweet. I would listen to my neighbor on the radio delivering the morning news as if he were talking to me across the fence.

Bad news followed when they sold the house. The family that moved in filed a newspaper report in short order to say how happy they were to live out in the country, where they could be free and let their children go naked. The woman announced in the same article that she had a stripper pole in the living room, for exer-cise. She later appeared at the door with only a towel around her waist when the yard men she had hired came for their check. The men reported to me that the couple had porn tapes for sale. This was conducted in a kind of garçonnière behind the main house. The little structure had a stained glass window salvaged from an old church, like a miniature clerestory window. I had always taken pleasure in seeing it there, facing my property, but now the sacred and the profane were forced into union and I was a daily witness.

After a number of run-ins, these people moved on, and the next couple were ideal. He was an infectious disease microbiologist and she a horticulturalist. No porn tapes out back. I offered to pay for a driveway to be installed entirely on their land in return for a revo-cation of the driveway easement. They were happy to have the new driveway; I was happy to have my land free of encumbrance.

Since then another amiable tenant has come and gone from the property. The current owners are newlyweds, open and more than friendly, continuing with the landscaping established earlier and adding their own garden. Good neighborhood citizens.

I have made peace with the neighbors who went into melt-down when the single-wide was set down within view of their bedroom window. To make matters worse, the new fence, while I had it set back from the boundary to allow them extra space, was still only fifty feet or so from their window. In the months following the single-wide's intrusion and the fence building, we had scorched-earth war.

Perhaps most dramatic was when the husband charged me with violating stream buffer codes. In my early days in the single-wide, I had set about cleaning up deadfall from Hurricane Fran along the creek with my chainsaw. When the county agent came to determine if I was guilty as charged, I happened to have in my favor a report from another county agency. In the process of cleaning up along the creek I had found an infected wild cherry tree, a limb of which I took to a county office. It was identified as a black knot fungus. I told them that it had also spread to a neighbor's trees across the creek, and they put out their edition of an all-points bulletin. I showed the stream buffer agent this report—evidence of my faultless virtue and alert citizenship—while he was examining the piles of deadfall. He found no problem and subsequently wrote a letter clearing me of all charges.

When the single-wide was hauled away, these neighbors opened their window and entertained us with music at high volume. But we have moved on and now exchange neighborhood gossip over the fence, I pay their daughter to water my porch plants when I am away, we trade head pats on our dogs, and try to forget when we acted like feral animals.

The regulatory environment of the county only adds to the anxiety of new homesteaders and the hair-trigger readiness to do battle with each other and long-settled residents. County codes present challenges at every turn when one is attempting to occupy land and put down roots. In my particular county—which hosts a university and where codes and matters of governance are informed largely by a sensibility dedicated to strict protection of place—architects and contractors have a running joke that codes not only require you to jump through hoops, but the hoops are set on fire.

When I occasionally drove across the land in my pickup during the single-wide days, I detected successive small ruts, a kind of palimpsest of rows from the days that Bowden cultivated a portion of the land. In one of his more approachable moods, he told me that sometimes it was a struggle, especially with flooding along the creek. He said he looked down there one day during a flood and his watermelons were floating away. That's when he decided to divert the creek. He dynamited it and made a dam with the loosened stones so that a new creek was formed, putting the flow farther from his cultivated land.

Today a dynamite blast would have county agents swarming the place, waving codes and covenants of all descriptions. Bowden would respond in the same way as when the agents came to tell him that runoff from his cattle feedlot was going into the creek and polluting the water reservoir. He told them they could kiss his ass.

I don't know what came of that violation. To put a spin on the idea of time's all-healing properties, we could say that the passing of years works to cure all violations and encroachments. Bowden's, mine, yours, those against my land, everyone's—including those of whoever made the hole in the single-wide floor, probably Ricky Wayne Stancil who defaulted on his loan and started the wars, his name on the repo order.

Dogs with Agency

She was a rescue dog and had no known name. Because it was the first place she sniffed out when I brought her home, I named her for the creek that is the back border of my land. Neville. A name usually reserved for males, but the naming of dogs is not necessarily governed by convention. The name can be whimsical, irrational, dedicated to a person or place, or drawn from a hat. And it will probably be capable of abbreviating. Or not. Spot. *See Spot run.* Or played upon: Neville answered to Nev-Nev, Nevy, even Noodle.

A veterinarian friend who was on duty at the rescue center had called to say that I should come see if I wanted this dog. They were euthanizing rescue dogs due to overcrowding. She said that she had taken one look at the dog in the lineup and knew that she could not put a needle in her. I went, saw her, and without the least hesitation fetched her straightway to my home. Saved her from what I call the needle line.

Neville was a mixed breed, but she had strong Boykin Spaniel features. Whit Boykin of South Carolina experimented with different breeds to develop a relatively small retriever, especially for working from a boat. *The dog that won't rock the boat.* To my amusement and joy, Neville rocked my boat every day for a number of years before she passed on.

Although she suffered with separation anxiety for a while when I first brought her home from the rescue center, she slowly came out of it. But initially, desperate to follow me when I left for work, she would literally bloody her claws trying to free herself from an enclosure I had arranged. Her anxiety apparently contributed to incontinence, so I could not leave her to roam freely in the single-wide trailer my then-wife and I were living in while our house was being built on this land.

The single-wide was a standard seventy feet long, and it afforded a freeway down the middle, from the study on one end, through the living room and kitchen, to the bedroom on the other end. Once Neville became comfortable with her new life, she would spontaneously light out running, using the freeway as a kind of race track, back and forth from one end to the other. She showed that same spontaneity and free spirit outside, running full tilt, wide circle after wide circle.

I could never determine her age. Nor could she tell me that or her original name. When she died, my friend Jane and I dug a grave for her beside my garden, put her on a bed of pine straw, and covered her. She is watched over by a small concrete angel that Jane gave me. To summon a touch of levity in hopes of assuaging the sadness of the occasion, we christened the angel as the Guardian Angel, given its proximity to the garden.

Jane says that Neville had an otherworldly quality. "I always doubted that she was a dog. She was certainly the least doggy dog I ever knew. I thought her a spirit, an Independent Spirit, in the form of a dog. She hailed from another dimension." I'm thinking that a needle line will do that. Alter the spiritual equation. No longer a doggy dog.

My current dog is an English Cocker Spaniel. It is commonly held that the name *cocker* comes from the association with the dog's hunting of woodcock in England. With limited success, I am trying to make a house dog out of a hunting dog. She will chase just about anything that moves—deer that appear out of the mist shrouding the creek bottom, squirrels that bury nuts in my porch planters, butterflies, skinks, on and on. The rabbit that comes out of the bushes every morning to graze drives her into a frenzy. I once had to prise from her mouth a small bird that she was trying to eat whole. It had flown against my window and was lifeless on the ground.

I named her Summa, a spin on the name of her sire Sumo. He was named Sumo because of his waddle as a puppy. I first saw him at my friends Charles and Tricia's place in Nova Scotia and was smitten immediately by his demeanor. Just before Charles and I departed for Quebec to fly-fish, Sumo brought a dead muskrat from the pond and placed it on the porch. When we arrived at the fishing lodge, Tricia called to say that she had tried to dispose of the muskrat but Sumo grabbed it and took it under the Tahoe. A dog with agency. That's when I asked Charles to put me on the list for a puppy if he bred Sumo.

Sumo is registered with the American Kennel Club. I had Summa spayed and since she would not be producing litters, valuable though they may have been, I did not register her. Had I registered her, she would be listed as Summa Cum Laude. Sumo's AKC papers show him to be Sumo of Seafields. Summa was sired by him with dam Nitro Proof Sky Blue. Or Skippy.

My former wife and I gave our sons a Corgi puppy one Christmas. The naming was simple enough—Saint Nicholas. Or Nicky. After we registered him with the AKC, I saw on his Litter Certificate that his forebears in the UK had names like Devereaux of Montjoy and so on. After the Atlantic crossing the progeny took on names that were truer to our republic. Cocoa Pebbles, for instance. The name Saint Nicholas, though, would seem to strike a fairer deal with the Devereaux.

Dogs with Agency

To be fair to the British, I should note that Queen Elizabeth II gave names such as Emma, Linnet, Willow, and Holly to her Corgis. That is not to say that the Corgis do not have more royal names listed with the UK Kennel Club. One of Elizabeth's early Corgis was registered as Windsor Loyal Subject. Another was registered as Hickathrift Pippa. She was called Susan, and according to an article in *Vanity Fair* she rode to Scotland, hidden under blankets, with Elizabeth on her honeymoon. Susan later gave birth to Sugar and Honey, who whelped Bee. Sugar was dam to Whisky and Sherry. In later years there was a tonal shift to less contrived names. What we commoners would call "hound names," such as Jet and Spark.

I have a "List of hounds owned by Paul J. Rainey Estate, Cotton Plant, Miss. Nov. 1, 1923" that provides a resonant sense of hound names. Buster, Queenie, Rattler, Rooster, Taters, Pearl, Light, Two Spot, the list goes on, fifty names, including an annotation for Claud: "After efect [sic] of distemper leaves them worthless."

Paul Rainey was a playboy and sportsman who, in addition to his huge estate in Mississippi, owned 26,000 acres in Vermilion Parish, Louisiana, near Avery Island, the McIlhenny's Tabasco headquarters. Rainey corresponded regularly with the maker of the iconic sauce, Ned McIlhenny, mostly about dogs and wildlife. (Rainey once sent McIlhenny a pony, and in return McIlhenny sent Rainey "two alligators, one 6 ft., one 7 ft." and on another occasion two coops of Mallard ducks. In a break from the exchange of animals, McIlhenny noted in his letter regarding the ducks that he was also shipping Rainey "a case each of shrimp, syrup, Creole Dinner, and fig preserves.")

It is notable how these men were keenly aware of dog names from each's kennel. And specific features. McIlhenny writes Rainey about one of Rainey's lost dogs, "the man I sent after the dog supposed to be 'Sandy' returned the dog, but I am sure it is not sandy [sic]. The dog is [a] heavy set hound with [a] big head and short heavy legs, blind in one eye but jet black, with the exception of the feet which are tan, and I never saw this dog in your pack." A week or so later, after McIlhenny has found the true Sandy and sent him to Rainey, Rainey replies, "I got old Sandy back alright, and was very glad to do it as I think a lot of the old fool."

For me, the most poignant instance of the separation of dog and master is Homer's account of Ulysses's return home after twenty years of absence. His old dog Argos recognizes him in his beggar's disguise in his approach to his home, where his wife Penelope's suitors are lying about, wining and dining on palatial fare, and bidding for Penelope's hand. Because Ulysses intends to slay the suitors, he cannot reveal that he knows Argos for fear his identity will become evident. As Ulysses passes by, the aged dog pricks his ears but hasn't the strength to drag himself toward Ulysses. He gives a thump of the tail and then breathes his last. Ulysses brushes away a tear and goes on to deal with the suitors.

I was not granted a farewell wag of the tail from my first dog, a gallant collie. He was hit by a car, and I did not discover his body until I returned home from school. I had picked his name from a hat four years earlier. Mike. I have no memory of the possible names in the hat nor any notion of how we came up with a name so utterly remote from names in my family or among my friends. But I welcomed the name and my new companion. A boy's dream. He joined in neighborhood games, accompanied me across the treacherous pasture on our way to the swimming hole, always gauging our distance from the bull that would charge us, ran beside my bike with great canine brio, played chase, chased balls, came when called.

To come when called. Mike. There alongside Devereaux, Hickathrift Pippa, the truant Sandy, Saint Nicholas, Neville, Argos, the others. And Summa in the host of the quick, alert to any call or motion. Each named with purpose, intent, albeit sometimes hidden or unknown.

The Adjustment of Claims

The woman said that she had pain and suffering from her infected finger and she wanted money for it. The infected finger, she claimed, was from working with the cheese at the cheese factory, which was insured for workers' compensation by the company I was employed by. The company was covering her medical bills, but she said that she was having pain and suffering and we owed her money for it. At my interview with her at the trailer park where she lived with her mother, I explained that workers' compensation does not cover pain and suffering. She said that her cousin was in a car wreck and he got money for his pain and suffering. That was not a case of workers' compensation, I told her, it was a case of personal injury and was settled in a torts claim. She said that she did not know anything about any torts but hers *was* a personal injury and she should get money.

She would get continued medical attention and compensation for lost work, I assured her. And if a doctor determined her infection caused partial disability, the medical team would help get her disabled finger rehabilitated. If a psychiatrist determined that she endured emotional distress, the psychiatric team would provide therapy. But I failed to convince her that she could not get paid for pain and suffering. Nor was the case settled while I was with the company.

While playing back a recording of the interview with the woman, I thought of my young uncle who had worked in a cheese factory during World War II. He was classified IV-F owing to a broken back in his medical records and was not qualified to serve in the military. The cheese was primarily intended for the war effort, but he would sometimes bring home a loaf of it tucked under his arm. He said they were not allowed to eat any on the job. We would sit at night and eat the war cheese with saltines, listening to the news. Pain and suffering everywhere.

After earning my undergraduate degree, I had decided to take a year off before graduate school. A prominent insurance company was recruiting on my undergraduate campus for a position in their claims department. I took my English major to them with the proposal that it qualified me perfectly for claims, what with the abetment of all the poems and novels I had deconstructed. They hired me, but not because of my literary wizardry. They just needed to get some boots on the claims ground.

They sent me to Boston for training in the basics of the adjustment process. There, with the other new hires, I was taught about investigating liability, assessing damages, reviewing medical or damage reports, and interviewing those involved—with a view to getting to claimants early before they lawyered up. Everything was pretty much in the service of protecting the interests of the insurance company. Lawyers, for the most part, call the company's negotiating method low-balling. But a given in negotiating claims, low-balling or not, is that it is almost always better to settle rather than go to court. Which is interminable, involving discovery, subpoenaing witnesses common and expert, the latter of whom usually have steep fees. As do the lawyers with their white boards, power points, and videos.

For relief from the intensity of the training sessions, my group and I took tours of Boston, invaded pubs, and distinguished ourselves as clueless outlanders. A measure of that limited world exposure was the day we decided to visit Harvard for the first time. We took the bus to Cambridge's Quincy Street bus stop and walked from there. As we approached what looked like Harvard in the near distance, we wondered aloud if that was in fact Harvard. One of our guys, nicknamed Hawkeye, said, "Hell yeah, that's Harvard. Look at all them fucking vines." It was indeed ivied Harvard and we were transfixed. Plebs among the Brahmins. But we were young and eager, and we went forth to our assigned cities to meet the world of claims.

Regarding the woman with the infected finger, I don't dismiss the reality of pain and suffering, but her pain, to whatever degree it existed, was not on the order of the gruesome accidents that do occur on the job. While pain is not covered in workers' compensation, there are schedules in the various state laws that place a value on body parts. Had she lost a thumb as a result of her infection, for example, state laws would typically figure her loss as follows: "For the loss of a thumb, sixty-six and two-thirds percent (66⅔%) of the average weekly wages during 75 weeks. The loss of more than one phalange shall be considered the loss of the entire finger or thumb: Provided, however, that in no case shall the amount received for more than one finger exceed the amount provided in this schedule for the loss of a hand."

The thumb gets special consideration because it is the highest-valued digit and the most important. Short of total loss, there are metrics for determining the degree of disability, from mild to marked: "In a mild defect (1) the tip of the thumb contacts the metacarpophalangeal joint (MCP) of the ring finger (3rd finger), but not the MCP of the pinky.— In a moderate defect (2) the tip of the thumb contacts the MCP of the middle finger (2nd finger), but not the MCP of the ring finger.— In a marked defect (3) the tip of the thumb contacts the MCP of the index finger (1st finger), but not the MCP of the middle finger."

I could quote further from the schedules to demonstrate the gradations in identifying disabilities—there are complicated entries ranging from metacarpophalangeal joints to miners' nystagmus—but they are so byzantine that the hyperbole of Dickens's *Bleak House* comes to mind. The case of Jarndyce and Jarndyce in the High Court of Chancery has gone on for generations and has "become so complicated that no man alive knows what it means."

Doyle's case, however, seemed pretty clear cut. He was working construction on the sly while drawing disability payments for full disability. Or at least that is the report that somehow came to my supervisor. Despite my negative feelings about snooping on fellow citizens—and because the company was signing the checks that would carry me to graduate school—I had to take a camera and go to the periphery of the job site to try to get pictures of Doyle working. He was on the job, going about normal work and generally behaving like an un-disabled man.

As it turned out, the attorney who represented him was a friend of my family, Cliff Finch. I was working out of the Memphis, Tennessee, office and Cliff's practice was some fifty miles away in my hometown in Mississippi. He greeted me in the way that family friends greet each other, but the transformation to his lawyer self, while both civil and jovial, was immediate when I told him that I was there to discuss Doyle's workers' compensation case. Cliff rose from his chair and gave his version of Doyle's bending down to pick up a heavy object at work, with Cliff catching his back as if in pain as he tried to assume an upright posture. Doyle's back popped like a rifle shot when he tried to stand straight, Cliff said, and he had to be taken to the hospital straightaway. Total disability ever since.

Trying to muster a level matter-of-fact tone without outright challenge to a family friend, I told Cliff that I had pictures of Doyle carrying bags of concrete, lifting rebar, and walking beams at a construction site the previous week. Cliff paused for the briefest of moments, and then seemingly without missing a beat, he asked, "Well, Jimmy, are they moving pictures?"

The Adjustment of Claims

It's not that the stills would have counted for nothing; Cliff was signaling to me that if the case went to court he would use every lawyerly tactic in his kit to establish Doyle's crippled self. I smiled and told him that he could get a medical update on Doyle's condition and we would discuss it on down the road. He knew and I knew that the case would never go to court. And Doyle would get a good settlement. I left for graduate school before the case was settled, and Cliff went on to the governor's mansion in Mississippi. No matter that we didn't see eye to eye on Doyle's condition; he continued in his friendship with me and my family. For instance, he named my father as one of his honorary colonels for his support in his campaign. During his campaign Cliff bagged groceries and carried a lunch pail, and once drove a bulldozer on a construction site. There are both stills and moving pictures to prove it.

Another case that was not resolved before I left the company is lodged strongly in my memory; owing not so much to any procedural matters as to a woman who appeared out of the darkness with a plea. Of which, more later.

There was an accident on the Mississippi River involving two tugboats, one of which my company insured for liability. I say "tugboat" to mean a tugboat and the array of barges that it is pushing, about 1,200 total footage in this case. Close to one-fourth of a mile of floating steel. Not a handily maneuverable conveyance.

There was damage, but the tugboat was able to continue downstream. No injuries or loss of life. I was to connect with the tugboat as it passed Memphis and interview the captain aboard the vessel. I knew nothing of admiralty laws, so I went to the library to read the maritime rules of the road, especially *Chapman Piloting & Seamanship*, "the Bible of Boating," which is still recommended for the US Coast Guard boating education classes.

The accident involved two vessels that were both going downstream, which meant that both vessels were considered "stand-on" vessels. A stand-on vessel has the right to keep going the way it is going, maintaining current speed. Since my man was attempting to pass the other vessel, his vessel, as I understood it, then became a "give-way" or "burdened vessel," with responsibility of signaling intentions to the stand-on vessel. If the give-way vessel intends to pass to starboard of the stand-on vessel, the give-way must blow one short blast; if passing to port the give-way must blow two short blasts. The stand-on responds in kind. Or issues five short and rapid blasts if she does not understand or if she feels the proposed maneuver is dangerous. Likewise the give-way may also issue these five blasts while overtaking.

Since the accident occurred at night, there was the factor of the angle of overtaking and the lighting: "A vessel shall be deemed to be overtaking when coming up with another vessel from a direction more than 22.5 degrees abaft her beam, that is, in such a position with reference to the vessel she is overtaking, that at night she would be able to see only the sternlight of that vessel but neither of her sidelights."

I had no idea if our captain had observed any of these regulations, though I have to say that cumulatively, as set forth in the International Regulations for Preventing Collisions at Sea, which apply to inland waters as well, the regulations made Dickens's Jarndyce and Jarndyce seem as simple as a child's alphabet book. What I decided was to ask only minimal questions and let the captain tell his story when I hooked up with his tugboat.

To do this I had to hire a pilot boat in Memphis to take me to connect with the tugboat. Since the tugboat could not just drop anchor in the Mississippi River while I conducted my interview, the hired boat would float alongside the tugboat as it made its way downstream toward New Orleans. In order to determine when the tugboat would be coming past Memphis, I had to rely on a ship-to-shore connection, there being no cell phones at that time. The captain told me that he would be coming past Memphis the next night.

Once I was on the hired boat, her skipper had radio communication and was able to identify the tugboat and damaged barges as they slid past, outlined on the half-mile-wide Mississippi. He pulled alongside and tied up. As I climbed aboard the tugboat, my

The Adjustment of Claims

hired skipper smiled as he waved me off, happy to have a floating holiday. I smiled back and offered the only nautical saying I knew. *Steady as she goes.*

Without my asking, the tugboat captain produced his license—and to add to his bona fides showed me a bar book, identifying sandbars along the Mississippi, that he had composed. He was a slender man with thinning hair, no other distinguishing features. Forget your rugged riverboat captain who walks with confidence among his crew, alternating between sternness and amiability. In addition to his unprepossessing person, his quarters reminded me of a cheap motel room—soiled carpet, bare walls, a nondescript desk, no books.

And there was the constant thrumming of the diesel engines. Whether that served as a kind of white noise aid or a harmful spectral density which entered his sleep I don't know. There are now special sleep clinics, such as the Vanderbilt Sleep Center, for tugboat captains, many of whom suffer with sleep apnea, and fatigue that comes from their schedule of six hours on, six hours off, as well as the boat's movement and noise.

I expected the captain to be nervous, but I was surprised when we got into the interview and he asked me to turn off my recorder for a moment. He went to a cabinet and took a long draw on a bottle of bourbon. He came back and we went on with the interview. Alcohol and drugs are forbidden on tugboats, so he was apparently willing to take the risk of bringing the bourbon aboard in secret. When I turned the recorder back on, I made no mention of the bourbon, though I noted it in my written report.

To establish my creds, I figured that I should pretend that I knew something about international navigation regulations, the ColRegs, so I asked about his approach to the other boat, did he fall within or outside the *22.5 degrees abaft her beam*, what about the visibility of her sternlight, the invisibility of her sidelights? What about the alertness and acuity of my insured captain?

Was I to believe that the other boat deviated from its course as he overtook it? And that he had sounded five short and rapid blasts on the boat's horn to no avail? And that indeed he was in total control of his vessel and its cargo? Maybe so. But finally how could I sort out the tangle of confusion on the water that night? One thing I was sure of, though; he would not inspire confidence on the witness stand if the case went to court.

While details of his person, his need for bourbon, his cabin, the thrumming of the diesels, remain relatively vivid, what I recall indelibly is the woman who appeared from a dimly lit recess on the deck and asked if she could come with me. I was at the railing waiting for help in reboarding the pilot boat.

Something about the plaintiveness of her request made it impossible for me to ask why or say no. She followed me over the railing onto the pilot boat. The look in her eyes in the stark deck lights, the slightness of her frame, how she seemed drawn inward, prompted the same response in the pilot boat captain. He nodded to me and turned the boat toward Memphis. She moved to a corner of the pilothouse, and I turned to watch the river, its slow flow, the passing lights of a distant tugboat and it barges headed downstream, the thrumming of its engines modulated across the water.

At that time, the mid-1960s, women would have been a rarity on tugboats, except maybe for an infrequent female cook. The woman did not fit my notion of a cook, whatever that was, and the captain had not mentioned that a female passenger needed to go ashore. Had he or some crew member brought her aboard openly or in secret? Had she done something to forfeit her berth? Or had she been mistreated? There were no bruises visible on her face. Her inwardness, her interiority, the set of her mouth, suggested that her story would remain with her until she got to a place where she could unburden herself of it. She pulled her dark coat tighter and lowered her head.

When we disembarked at Memphis around dawn, she offered a barely audible thank-you and walked away. No request for a ride, no appeal for money. Without any pondering back and forth of what her story might have been, I bid farewell to the pilot boat captain— my lame *steady as she goes* falling short of the moment—and went home to sleep. I had no hint of what claim she had in life, or what damage she may have caused, or suffered. Just that she had boarded a boat with me, a stranger, in the dark and had gone to wherever I was going.

Like the cases of the woman with the infected finger and the putatively disabled Doyle, nothing was settled in the tugboat case before I left the company. There were plenty of cases that I did settle, however, before going off to parse stories and poems for whatever meaning I could find. The stated doctrine in claims is that the claimant is to be made whole. In damage cases it is possible, more or less, to determine loss, though those cases can be contentious. In medical cases, the matter is usually contentious.

In an attempt to gauge degrees of pain, one law firm has a pain scale from one to ten and a chart with emoji-like figures, one of which a claimant is to mark—smiley face to scowl with tears. Our pain quantified, made visible.

Ghost Beads

To go into Canyon de Chelly on the Navajo Reservation in northern Arizona, with the exception of one hiking trail, you must be escorted by a park ranger or an authorized Navajo guide. I called a Navajo guide service and booked a tour with the young owner. When I showed up in the parking lot of the Best Western in Chinle, Arizona, on the morning of my tour, I was met by a man with a long ponytail driving a beat-up four-wheel-drive Ford F-150. David (not his real name) was the father of the owner, and he was in no mood to show me the canyon. Evidently his son had overbooked and had called on his father to substitute. I was concerned that the son was not my guide, but I knew not to express my concern. David was already in a foul mood.

Instead of laying out the day's plan, he asked me, in a challenging tone, what I wanted to see. As luck would have it, I had done some research, and I told him that I was particularly interested in Antelope House Ruin and White House Ruin, and of course his normal tour. I added, with secret satisfaction in my research, that I knew that the famous Spider Rock was too far into the canyon for our tour. I could see it the next day by driving to the overlook on the South Rim and looking down on its 800-foot sandstone spire.

We registered at the visitor center and headed back to David's truck. When we got back to the truck, I told David to hold up a minute, I had forgotten to get a visitor brochure with a map. "You don't need one; I know everything you need to know." With that, he headed for the road into the canyon in silence. I wanted a map to get a visual impression of our route, but I did not say anything. I thought to myself, though, "How am I going to spend the whole day with this man?"

Engaging the four-wheel drive for the deep, dry sand of Chinle Wash as we entered the canyon, David was preoccupied with negotiating the sand so that we did not get stuck. I had read that the guides readily pulled fellow guides out if they hit impassable sand and were stalled there. After we made it through that passage, David began telling of the sites we passed, though his descriptions had a hint of rote. A patch of green prompted him to comment on how the ancients planted vegetables in addition to their hunting and then he cataloged the vegetables—corn, beans, squash, and so on—in a rather mechanical way. This rote was more or less necessary, I realized later, given the numerous times he made the same delivery to clients. As we went along he called my attention to details—the heights of the canyon walls that increased as we got deeper into the canyon—some reaching as high as 1,000 feet—the cut and striated colors, the particular petroglyphs that he slowed or stopped for: Native American hunters on stick-like horses chasing antelopes, a hand, a man with an oversized phallus, zig-zag lines representing a river, lightning, or a snake, there are different interpretations, depending on the context.

In addition to these images of the basic effort at survival and the identification of the human world, the petroglyphs—here and in other ancient American Indian sites—also include symbols and totems that posit a spiritual world, mysticism, mystery. Spirals interpreted to mean eternity or life's journey, sunrays indicating constancy, the thunderbird symbolizing unending happiness, and so forth. Jungians and those studying the collective unconscious find fertile ground in these remnants.

Though interpretations vary as to its meaning, some say that the incomplete swastika on the cliff wall at Antelope House Ruin suggests a migration story—the four corners of the earth. Other candidates are well-being, use in healing rituals, the land as abiding presence, a whirling log. Still, the swastika can be unsettling, given its contemporary association. Or at least it was for me. Which speaks to the power of symbol.

Ansel Adams visited Canyon de Chelly several times, but I cannot determine the circumstances surrounding his photograph of Antelope House Ruin in 1942. His photograph is of a portion of the ruin where the swastika is not visible. The portion Adams chose to photograph was of course a function of his artistic judgment, what his eye told him to frame and have the camera capture. My guess is that one consideration in his choice was that the swastika would command undue attention, especially in 1942, and become the focus. Whereas what he chose for his photograph—in its contrast between the native architecture and the natural textures and sheerness of the rock cliff—evokes a sense of mystery and human effort in the face of seemingly impossible odds.

Nor can I determine, by comparing Adams's photograph to a photograph that I took of the ruin, the exact portion shown in Adams's photograph. The ruin itself is now protected by fencing, so the visitor cannot approach for a close view and must depend on binoculars, which I did not have, or photographs later. The excavations done in 1970–73 should not have affected the view. That I cannot find the exact locus of Adams's photograph, even looking at views of the ruin from above—the South Rim—is a cipher. Which for me gives Adams's gelatin silver print all the more allure and mystery.

When we arrived at White House Ruin near the base of a sheer cliff some 500 feet high, we stopped at a vendor's stand serving refreshments in the shade of cottonwood trees. The stand was marked by a US flag and a sign with red lettering listing frybread, beverages, and candy. Both flag and sign stood out unnaturally against the colors of the canyon and the ancient architecture, though the White House takes its name from the white plaster coating the long back wall of the upper dwelling. The National Park Service tells us that the White House was constructed and occupied between 1060 AD and 1275 AD. It is a part of the remains of cultures that go back nearly 5,000 years—Archaic, Basketmaker, Puebloan, and Hopi. The most recent are the Navajo, or Diné, which is their cultural name. Their predecessors are often called Anasazi, the "ancient ones."

According to an NPR interview, Ansel Adams took his son Michael into the canyon with him when he photographed White House Ruin in 1942, the same date as his photograph of Antelope House Ruin. Michael had this to say of that venture: "It's a stunning image of this sandstone wall with the water scarring on it and the ruin against the very black background. We had to climb down into the canyon and wade the river to get over to take this picture. It was stunning. I remember the heat more than anything else because we had to walk back through the river and climb to the top with all of his big cameras."

Speaking of heat, I bought a bottle of water at the vendor's stand at White House Ruin, but when I declined the Navajo frybread, a deep-fried dough, the vendor's neutral look changed to one of vague disapproval. I did not want to eat fried food that I was new to and risk an unsettled stomach or added thirst in the heat of the rest of the tour. But I figured that to try to explain would be to seal my status as white man wuss. David remained silent and ate his frybread.

He was more talkative, however, when we resumed our tour. As it turned out, part of his reticence and negative attitude was owing to the departure the night before of the woman he had been living with for a long while. A Swedish woman, improbable as it would seem, a relationship involving such disparate societies, but I had no reason to doubt him. He didn't say why she left, but I assumed it was like the failure of any relationship. Each one unique, but all sharing the same fact of failure. I told him that I had gone through a divorce and could understand his feelings of loss and sadness. He seemed to buck up a bit in this assurance that he was not alone in suffering dejection. Not that he implied we were companions in an emotional shambles; he had simply given voice to what he was feeling. He then drove on in silence.

As though it were coincidence, we came to a portable table, set up against a backdrop of small boulders, where a woman had her wares on display. My thought was that David probably had an arrangement with her for a cut of any sales he directed her way, but I put that suspicion aside and gave over to my interest in the jewelry and craft items that she had for sale, especially the jewelry containing turquoise. I bought a necklace with an alternating series of small turquoise pieces. Considering its modest price, I suspected that it was made of paste jewels from China or somewhere. But it did not matter, I told myself. This woman was trying to make a living on a reservation that offered little hope.

I had no need for another necklace—I had no need for *any* necklace, for that matter—but I was so fascinated by the story behind those of hollowed juniper berries or ghost beads that I bought one. Berries fall to the ground, ants chew off one end, and eat the inside. The berries are then collected and dried. The woman said they protected one from evil spirits, bad dreams, ghosts, but when she held up the necklace to show me, it separated at the clasp and some of the ghost beads spilled onto her table. She rounded up the beads as if nothing had happened, threaded them back on the necklace, repaired the clasp, and handed the necklace to me. David jumped back, a ghost in mock fright. His only show of humor during the entire tour.

So David had now lightened up even more. Not exactly buoyant, but less burdened. He asked me if I knew Johnny Depp. I told him that I didn't know Johnny Depp personally but I had seen him in movies. David then said, with a note of pride, that he was one of the guides during the filming of scenes of *The Lone Ranger* that took place in Canyon de Chelly. Johnny Depp was Tonto. David preferred him in that role over Jay Silverheels in previous versions. One would think that David's preference was because of his connection as guide with the Depp film, but David said that he was won over by Depp's comments about Native Americans. "I started thinking about Tonto," Depp had said, "and what could be done in my own small way to . . . attempt to take some of the ugliness thrown on the Native Americans, not only in *The Lone Ranger*, but the way Indians were treated throughout [the] history of cinema, and turn it on its head." Depp stated that he wanted to play Tonto not as a sidekick to the Lone Ranger but as a warrior and as a man of great integrity and dignity. David did not care for the taxidermy crow that Depp wore as headdress, however. He preferred the way Jay Silverheels was portrayed: headband with hair in a braid.

Whether or not Depp altered the Hollywood stereotype of American Indians is controversial. In his support, for instance, Depp was made an honorary son and member of the Comanche tribe. Others say he presented old clichés. "After all these years and all this effort to try to get Hollywood to understand their portrayal of Native Americans, and some real good work having been accomplished, to see it all sort of pushed aside because a big star wants to play Tonto," says Hanay Geiogamah, a Kiowa tribe member and UCLA professor. "Further hardening . . . the notion that Hollywood just ain't ever going to get it right. The movies are never going to do right by the Indians." But don't try to tell David that. Except as regards the dead crow.

I bring up this Hollywood episode because there's a questionable aspect in David's embrace of Depp and his Tonto. His boasting of his part in guiding Depp and his crew in Canyon de Chelly, along with his ready acceptance of outsiders and income that Hollywood brought, was inconsistent with the undercurrent of resentment over the white man's coming onto reservation land. At any rate that is what I felt at the onset of my tour, a negative undercurrent, though I can understand the sense of intrusion, the memory of events such as battles with Spanish colonists—which some of the petroglyphs and pictographs depict—and the Long Walk, that expulsion following Kit Carson's campaign in 1864 against the Navajo, the humiliation and extreme hardship during the many years before they were allowed to return home, albeit a reservation.

I had experienced this resentment before in various foreign places. There is one's vague paranoia, of course, but the wrongs of past colonial rule are a reality, particularly in the Caribbean, as is the neocolonial animosity toward those wrongs. This reality is similar to the enmity over the taking of land from the American Indians and the poverty on the reservations, mixed with desire for any money coming in. But what is wrenching to witness is the stress between that animosity—perhaps it is mixed with resignation—at our being there and the need for the money we bring. I don't want to paint with too broad a brush, but there are psychological consequences in the dichotomy between resentment and supplication, or petition, for our dollars. The latter may be in the dependence on tourist money in order to have a job.

On the island of Virgin Gorda I intended a show of deference in addressing as "Captain" the operator, a British Virgin Islander, of the Boston Whaler in which he was delivering me to the small uninhabited island of Little George for a day of snorkeling. He was quick to tell me that his name was Trevor, indicating that I was not to address him as Captain, which he apparently took as disregard for his identity, his sense of self. He did not smile or give any indication of understanding that my address was an attempt at respect and courtesy. Nor did he establish any eye contact on the way out or on the way in when he came to fetch me that afternoon. But his job was dependent on the revenue of tourists such as myself.

Once as I was walking along a sidewalk with other tourists on St. Martin, a native of the island struck me in the jaw with a homemade crutch that she raised in a fake move of changing the position of her crutch. Her look of ill will toward me was unmistakable. A fellow citizen of hers knew that she had done it intentionally and he scolded her. Whether he acted out of a sense of decency or an attempt to avoid threats to tourism I do not know. Though there was no physical act, I could feel the antagonistic stares of Jamaicans once when I was in one of their farmers' markets. Likewise the stares of Native Americans when I have driven through reservations, particularly the one for the Makah Tribe at the end of the Olympic Peninsula. That I was driving a late model rental car and obviously observing them only added to the sense of intrusion.

When we arrived back at the Best Western after the tour, David was again reticent, and I could sense that he was preoccupied with the departure of the woman that he had been accustomed to going home to. He had told me that his brother was an alcoholic but that he was not. Still and all, I knew that if he went to an empty home he would brood and quite possibly fall into deeper depression. I told him that he should not be alone, that he should go to family or friends. And talk to them. Not drink, not give in to hurtful behavior.

After we got out of the truck, he walked across the parking lot toward the restaurant adjacent to the Best Western to get some coffee. He looked back at me, and I could tell from the look on his face and his body language—not exactly surrender but a giving over—that he had taken in the counsel I offered. I had become the guide. The white man without a map. The white man who didn't eat the frybread. The white man with the ghost beads.

Bathing the Buddha Man

He has been sitting there it seems forever beneath the bonsai, waiting with his line in the water for whatever comes along. His fishing pole is a pine needle. It was almost indistinguishable among its pine needle fellows on the ground in front of my house, then I detected its slight curve. Perfect. Initially I had inserted a round toothpick in his hand, or rather in the hole where his original fishing pole had rested. That pole had been lost before he came to my house. The toothpick, though, was out of scale and lacked the limberness of the pine needle. And in my mind the toothpick came off as too alert, too set on success. None of this is to imply that the Buddha Man himself is unaware of what is going on in the water that I imagine in slow flow before him. I have to imagine also the fishing line and whatever bait he has chosen.

I brought the bonsai to my house during the time my former wife Lee and I were cleaning out the apartment of our son Josh, who had died of heart failure at age thirty-three, following a long period of mental illness and medication. He had placed it on the window sill above his sink. It was a miniature ficus. After admiring a bonsai of mine, he had been prompted to get one of his own. But his was more elaborately potted—an oval vase and a special potting mix substrate. Seated next to an upright piece of diminutive bamboo and a pebble representing a small boulder was the calm ceramic figure in the shade of the bonsai, looking out at the water. I named him the Buddha Man, though he looks like a cross between a Zen master and Buddha.

Josh once told me that if you learn that a plant you have given someone dies you feel terrible. Though he had given it to me unawares, that is what happened to the bonsai. It died. Since Josh was not there to feel terrible, I felt terrible for him. Throughout the time that I watered it, a few of the small leaves would yellow and drop. And I would panic. But I would sprinkle some Osmacote fertilizer on it and continue to water it weekly. I called the light sprinkle from the watering spout *bathing the Buddha Man*. Over the years, though, root rot set in—or perhaps it became root-bound—and it dropped its last yellow leaf. The Buddha Man maybe took notice of the lack of shade, but his study of the water has remained constant.

In likening the poet's autumn in life to leaves on a tree, Shakespeare arranges the leaves in a particular order:

> When yellow leaves, or none, or few, do hang
> Upon those boughs. . . .

I have always admired the sequence of that passage, Shakespeare's arranging the syntax—and keeping with the iambic rhythm—so that *none* comes almost illogically before *few*. Playing down the finality of *none*. Allowing a bit more time.

But the bonsai had run out of time. So too had Josh. Though the bonsai is now dead, I have left it on the bookshelf below my window, always making sure that the Buddha Man's fishing pole is loosely secure in his hand. Who knows what might come along?

Acknowledgments

Thanks go out first to Bland Simpson, who suggested to the Press that they ask to see a collection of my essays. Fortune was smiling, for I had just put together a collection. The Press requested to see it, I sent it in straightway, and here it is a year and change later. A book, thanks to Bland.

How that book shaped up is owing greatly to the staff at the University of North Carolina Press, particularly to my editor Lucas Church, his assistant Thomas Bedenbaugh, and project editor Valerie Burton.

For further thanks I'm going to use the traditional abecedarian order in hopes of softening the feelings of those who are scrambling to get priority shoutouts in such a list—though granted that some deserve extra special thanks for keen critical eyes and ears, general spiritual support, and long-standing friendship.

John Anderson, Elizabeth Arroyo, Barbara Bennett, Betsy Bennett, Walter Bennett, Roy Blount Jr., Susan Blount, Marshall

Chapman, Michael Chitwood, Elizabeth Cox, Hal Crowther, Gerald Duff, Bill Ferris, Marcie Ferris, Richard Ford, Charles Gaines, Patricia Gaines, Marianne Gingher, Joan Griswold, Allan Gurganus, Dan Halpern, Ed Hirsch, Fred Hobson, Roger Hodge, Jane Holding, Richard Howorth, Tom Huey, Danielle Amir Jackson, Jay Jennings, Duck Johnston, Lillias Johnston, Will Johnston, Rodney Jones, Virginia King, Sally Mann, Carroll Mayfield, Dan Mayfield, Jill McCorkle, Michael McFee, Tom McGuane, Joanne Prichard Morris, David Payne, Adelaide Probst, Cliff Probst, Alex Rankin, Sarah Rankin, Tom Rankin, Ron Rash, Ellen Rosenbush, Page Seay, Samia Serageldin, Jackie Sergi and all my Mississippi folks, Alan Shapiro, Ann Simpson, Lee Smith, Pat Stephens, George Terll, Liza Terll, Daniel Wallace, Curtis Wilkie, Cary Wolfe, Elizabeth Woodman.

I don't know what happened to the XYZs. I guess I could thank Xenophon whose *Anabasis* I went through line by line in Greek class and learned all about hoplites, satraps, and darics. A story helpful in understanding when to go forward, when to back up, and when to leave. Come! Come! Where? Where?